WILLIAM E. NELSON

Marbury

v.

Madison

The Origins and Legacy of Judicial Review

UNIVERSITY PRESS OF KANSAS

Published by the University Press of Kansas (Lawrence, Kansas 66049), which was organized by the Kansas Board of Regents and is operated and funded by Emporia State University, Fort Hays State University, Kansas State University, Pittsburg State University, the University of Kansas, and Wichita State University.

Library of Congress Cataloging-in-Publication Data

Nelson, William Edward, 1940–

Marbury v. Madison : the origins and legacy of judicial review / William E. Nelson

p. cm. — (Landmark law cases & American society)

Includes bibliographical references and index.

ISBN 0-7006-1061-8 (cloth : alk. paper) — ISBN 0-7006-1062-6 (pbk. : alk. paper)

1. Judicial review—United States—History. 2. Separation of powers—United States—History. 3. Marbury, William, 1761 or 2-1835—Trials, litigation, etc. 4. Madison,

James, 1751-1836—Trials, litigation, etc. I. Title. II. Series.

KF4575 .N45 2000

347.73'12—dc21   00-043472

British Library Cataloguing in Publication Data is available.

Printed in the United States of America

10 9 8 7 6 5 4 3 2

The paper used in this publication meets the minimum requirements of the American National Standard for Permanence of Paper for Printed Library Materials z39.48-1984.

TO MAY VOGELBACHER

AND THE MEMORY OF

GUS VOGELBACHER

CONTENTS

EDITORS' PREFACE

At first glance, one might wonder why such an old chestnut as *Marbury v. Madison* would merit inclusion in a modern series on landmark cases. After all, the doctrine that the highest court in the land has the duty as well as the authority to decide on the constitutionality of federal and state legislation is not only almost two hundred years old, it has been confirmed innumerable times. The case itself was decided by a unanimous court and did not bring about a revolution in the legal system or the politics of the times. Indeed, its author, Chief Justice John Marshall, crafted it to avoid a direct encounter between the Federalists on the United States Supreme Court and President Thomas Jefferson and his new Republican majority in Congress.

The fact remains that the case is an essential part of the adolescence of American democratic republicanism, for in it the Court upheld the rule of law without calling into question the electoral revolution that turned the Federalists out of office and brought in the Jeffersonian Republicans. Marshall and his court also protected the independence of the judiciary and the High Court at a time when these institutions were under attack. Thus the legacy of the case is not only its doctrinal contribution of judicial review to American constitutionalism but its proof that the Court could remain, if not above all political considerations, at least safe from overt partisanship.

This was no easy task, for as Professor Nelson so incisively demonstrates, Marshall faced two dangers. The first was the Republican animus for a Federalist-dominated judiciary. The second was the temptation to use the courts to further the Federalist program. This included a strong central government and strong courts. Marshall succumbed to neither the fear of the first nor the allure of the second. By insisting upon the traditional view that the task of courts was one of discovering rather than making law, he placed the decision of the Court out of the reach of both parties.

But later American courts, in a different political context, have changed the way in which judicial review functions. In an age when the consensus that eighteenth-century Anglo-American elites shared has given way to the politics of interest groups, Nelson argues, we have come to see courts as policy-making bodies weighing the competing interests behind the cases brought to the bar. Thus, for us, judicial review becomes something that would be quite foreign to Marshall—a final balancing of the interests.

This is an exciting book, broad in scope and daring in conception. It combines legal history, constitutional theory, and political science. In a final chapter, Nelson goes beyond the boundaries of the United States to apply the lessons of *Marbury* to nations that did not exist when Marshall handed down his decision. For now these new states face the same issues of law and politics, constitutionalism and partisanship, that Marshall understood so well.

ACKNOWLEDGMENTS

My work on this book, as well as the articles from which parts of it are derived, has resulted in the accumulation of many debts. The research staff of the New York University Law Library fulfilled every request for materials that I presented to it, and the Nassau County Public Library System, which has an excellent American history collection, was equally helpful. I am especially indebted to Ronald Brown and Elizabeth Evans, reference librarians at the NYU Law Library, and to Jeffrey Mason, the reference librarian at the Hewlett-Woodmere Public Library.

I also wish to acknowledge permission to reprint portions of the following articles:

William E. Nelson, "The Eighteenth-Century Background of John Marshall's Constitutional Jurisprudence," *Michigan Law Review* 76 (1978), 893.

William E. Nelson, "History and Neutrality in Constitutional Adjudication," *Virginia Law Review* 72 (1986), 1237.

William E. Nelson, "Changing Conceptions of Judicial Review: The Evolution of Constitutional Theory in the States, 1790–1860," *University of Pennsylvania Law Review* 120 (1972), 1166.

A draft of this book was presented to the Legal History Colloquium at New York University School of Law, and I am indebted to all its participants for their helpful comments and criticisms, but especially to Mark Brilliant, Barry Friedman, William LaPiana, and Howard Venable. My colleagues Christopher Eisgruber and Larry Kramer each contributed in significant ways to the refinement of my thinking as I transformed the earlier articles into the book, and my former colleague Bruce Ackerman made even more significant contributions to the ideas that appeared in those early articles. The late Edward Weinfeld, himself a judge of the same Olympian qualities as John Marshall, had for years urged me to turn my article on Marshall's constitutional jurisprudence into a book, and he thereby had made me especially receptive when Peter Hoffer offered me the opportunity to do so. Hoffer's patient editing substantially improved the book, as did the reader's report of G. Edward White.

I also owe an unredeemable debt to John Sexton, who has made New York University School of Law the best place in the world for the scholarly study of law in general and of legal history in particular. Generous support for the writing of this book was provided by the Filomen D'Agostino and Max E. Greenberg Faculty Research Fund of New York University School of Law. I thank Lisa Mihajlovic for her work on final preparations of the manuscript.

As always, I must thank my family—my wife, Elaine, and my children, Leila and Gregory—for the many sacrifices they make that enable me to work as a scholar. This book is also my opportunity to thank two other family members: May Vogelbacher and her late husband, Gus Vogelbacher, a man of Marshallian talent who devoted his life, as John Marshall always wanted to devote his, to his family and to anyone else who needed his help. Even before I married into their family, I had been the beneficiary of their help and generosity, which began when I was in third grade and May Vogelbacher was my teacher and which continues to this day.

Introduction

Marbury v. Madison will long remain a foundational case for understanding the work and jurisprudence of the Supreme Court of the United States. In an 1803 opinion by Chief Justice John Marshall, the Court explicitly ruled for the first time that it possessed what we now call the power of judicial review, or jurisdiction to examine whether legislation enacted by Congress is consistent with the Constitution. Upon examination, the Court declared section 13 of the Judiciary Act of 1789 unconstitutional and therefore null and void. Following *Marbury,* the Supreme Court did not assert its power of judicial review for another 54 years. During the last 150 years, however, the Court has invalidated numerous acts of Congress, and during the last 50 years, constitutional courts throughout the world have often emulated the American court by declaring acts of their own legislatures void.

Thus, *Marbury v. Madison* was a truly seminal case, which ultimately has conferred vast power on the Supreme Court of the United States and on other constitutional courts throughout the world. What makes the case even more important is the absence of any clear plan on the part of the Constitution's framers to provide the Court with this power. The convention that drafted the Constitution in Philadelphia during the summer of 1787 had left no doubt that the Supreme Court would have authority to invalidate state laws that were contrary to the Constitution, and Congress, in turn, effectuated the Philadelphia Convention's determination when, in the Judiciary Act of 1789, it gave the Court jurisdiction to hear appeals from state-court judgments that had rejected claims based on the federal Constitution.

The power of the Court to review laws passed by Congress, on the other hand, had been left indeterminate. The possibility of the Court's exercise of this power had been mentioned at the Convention and discussed during the ratification debates, and some state courts had already asserted an analogous power to review the acts of their own legislatures. But the power of judicial review was somewhat controversial in 1787 and 1788, and no effort was made in connection with the adoption of the federal Constitution to get the controversy resolved. The framers left its resolution to the future, and some fifteen years later, *Marbury v. Madison* resolved it.

Today we understand that, in deciding whether or not to invalidate an act of a coordinate legislative body, a court inevitably must choose between competing social policies. We believe, for example, that when the Supreme Court decides whether to allow Congress to adopt a law giving members of designated racial groups a specified percentage of all contractual business with the federal government, the Court must choose between competing policies of equal justice—one that treats all individuals equally without regard to race and another that seeks to create equality by giving preferential treatment to people likely to have been victimized by past discrimination.

This tenet that constitutional decisions by the Supreme Court typically involve policy choice originated in progressive and legal-realist critiques of the Court early in the twentieth century. Over time these critiques resulted in what, until recently, has remained the conventional wisdom about *Marbury*, judicial review, and the Marshall Court. This conventional wisdom, articulated by progressive historians and legal scholars ranging from Albert Beveridge, Robert G. McCloskey, and J. M. Sosin to Felix Frankfurter and Charles Warren, contends that John Marshall, in deciding *Marbury*, consciously furthered the political goals of the Federalist Party, to which he had belonged—first, by stretching the Constitution's meaning to increase national power at the expense of state power, and second, by designing constitutional doctrines, such as judicial review, that protected the upper classes' privileges against the growing democratic onslaught that in 1829 finally placed Andrew Jackson in the White House.

Frankfurter arguably expressed the conventional view most

clearly when he declared in his 1937 book, *The Commerce Clause under Marshall, Taney and Waite*, that the deepest article of Marshall's faith was the need for a strong central government, not because the Constitution requires it but because such a government would become "the indispensable bulwark of the solid elements of the nation." This conventional wisdom continues even today to claim adherents. In one recent article, for example, Christopher Eisgruber has advanced an eloquent argument that Marshall's interpretation of the Constitution as a bulwark of national judicial power reflected a policy judgment that the national judiciary was an institution well suited to promoting the happiness and prosperity of the American people.

Nonetheless, during the past two decades, the conventional wisdom has begun to erode. Beginning with my own essay, "The Eighteenth-Century Background of John Marshall's Constitutional Jurisprudence," historians have advanced new explanations by focusing on what, once it is stated, is obvious: that Marshall and his contemporaries, like all historical actors, understood only the world in which they grew to maturity and could not foresee the future. As James O'Fallon has observed, we need to understand *Marbury* as a case "born of the bitter political battle of its time" and should not credit its author, Chief Justice Marshall, "with foresight that would honor an oracle." If we are to comprehend *Marbury* and the Marshall Court, in short, we need to situate them in the context of eighteenth-century legal and political theory, not in the ideological matrix of twentieth-century progressivism and legal realism.

It must be stated emphatically that few, if any, Americans in the decades before and after 1800 believed that policy choice was an inherent element in judicial decision making. Such was not the understanding of the framers who drafted the Constitution at the Philadelphia Convention in 1787 or secured its ratification during the year thereafter. Nor was it the understanding of the Marshall Court when it handed down *Marbury v. Madison*. The framers of the Constitution and the justices who decided *Marbury* understood that only an entity possessing sovereignty—that is, the power to make the ultimate policy choices inherent in changing or creating law—could resolve policy questions. Courts, which did not possess sovereignty, could only find the law as it already existed.

Moreover, political thinkers in late-eighteenth-century America had been witness to a decades-long battle over the proper location of sovereignty, a battle that had culminated in war and other momentous political events. Classical British political theory, especially as articulated by William Blackstone in his leading treatise, *Commentaries on the Laws of England*, which was published during the 1760s, posited that sovereignty lay with the King in Parliament: that is, only the House of Commons, the House of Lords, and the crown, acting together in conjunction, could change the law by enacting legislation. But when Parliament gave vent to this theory in the Declaratory Act of 1766, which stated that the King in Parliament could make laws binding on its American colonies in all cases whatsoever, Americans objected. In their view, Parliament could not be their sovereign, since they lacked representation therein.

For the next nine years, Britain persisted in its claim of parliamentary sovereignty over its colonies, and Americans persisted in their rejection of the claim. Finally, in 1776, they declared their independence. Although the Declaration of Independence did not definitively establish the locus of sovereignty, most Americans of the Revolutionary generation assumed that sovereignty lay in the newly independent state legislatures.

Granting full sovereignty to the states, however, left the national government weak, and by the mid-1780s leaders who would come to be known as Federalists began a campaign that culminated in the drafting and ratification of the federal Constitution and in the establishment in 1789 of the federal government. During that campaign, they frequently had to address the issue of sovereignty. They could not leave sovereignty with the states, since state sovereignty made the national government too weak, nor could they place sovereignty in the national government, since Americans who had fought a Revolutionary War against a centralized sovereign government remained too fearful of power to establish a new sovereign national state. During the ratification debates, some Federalists made the intellectual leap of urging that sovereignty lay with the people, not with any governmental body.

There is no need for purposes of this book to resolve the question of where, in the view of most Americans in the early 1800s, sovereignty—the power to make or change law through the resolution of issues of social policy—lay. If any institution of government was thought in 1803 to possess sovereignty, surely it was not the Supreme Court of the United States. Thus, no one could have thought that the Court, in asserting the power of judicial review, was assuming jurisdiction to make the choices of social policy that only a sovereign could make. In deciding *Marbury v. Madison*, Chief Justice Marshall and his colleagues thus were doing something other than adopting judicial review as we now know it at the beginning of the twenty-first century.

Recent historians and constitutional theorists have offered several suggestions about what the Marshall Court was doing, all of which capture part of reality. One useful book by Charles Hobson, who has been working for many years on a multivolume edition of John Marshall's papers, situates *Marbury* and Marshall's career in the shift from the classical republican political culture of the Revolutionary era, which emphasized the good of the community as a whole, to a liberal political culture emphasizing individual rights and freedom, which was more or less in place by 1840. Most historians probably would reject Hobson's thesis, since the current wisdom in the profession doubts whether eighteenth-century republicanism differed enough from nineteenth-century liberalism to give either concept much explanatory power. Even if one accepts the current wisdom, however, Hobson's book still has special value as a result of the author's access to information about John Marshall, his Court, and his jurisprudence that no other scholar possesses.

Sylvia Snowiss has authored a second book that places Marshall's *Marbury* decision in a late-eighteenth-century context. Her argument draws a distinction between ordinary law, which she claims was routinely enforced in the courts, and fundamental law, such as a constitution, which, in her view, could not be enforced by courts but only by electoral or other political action, ultimately by revolution. Snowiss is surely correct in recognizing that important leaders, such as Thomas Jefferson, author of the Declaration of Independence and future president, understood that the people themselves could enforce fundamental law—a view most Americans no longer hold. But, as we shall see in Chapter 1, she underestimates the role of popular law finding, through the institution of the jury, in the enforcement of ordinary law. Moreover, her distinction, although useful in explaining why the doctrine of judicial review enunciated in *Marbury v. Madison* differed radically from the sort of judicial review practiced by courts today, does not identify the element in the eighteenth-century background of *Marbury* that enabled John Marshall to assert, as he did, the power of the Supreme Court to enforce fundamental law. Snowiss's book, in the end, thus offers a strong, implicit critique of the sort of broad-ranging, policy-oriented judicial review practiced by many constitutional courts today, rather than an explanation of how the practice came into being historically.

A third book, by Robert Lowry Clinton, does offer such an explanation. Clinton interprets *Marbury* in light of Blackstone's principles of statutory construction, the most relevant of which allowed judges to ignore a statute if its application would result in absurdity, repugnancy, or impossibility of performance, but denied the judiciary power to revise or repeal statutes on grounds of policy. Clinton establishes that American ideas about judicial power at the time of *Marbury* were consistent with Blackstone's principles and that those ideas changed, so as to allow judicial invalidation of legislation on constitutional policy grounds, only at the end of the nineteenth century.

In this book, I do not disagree with Clinton's interpretation. I do not question that Blackstonian analytical principles were in the air at the time the Supreme Court decided the *Marbury* case, nor do I question whether those principles played a role in the decision. I have no doubt that the analytical tools available to judges help to determine the arguments and language they use in resolving cases.

But my goals and interests in this book are different. Unlike prior scholars like Sylvia Snowiss and the progressive historians, I am not striving to evaluate whether the Marshall Court usurped power or otherwise made a wrong decision in asserting the power of judicial review in *Marbury*. Like Snowiss, as well as Clinton and Hobson, I do believe that judicial review in *Marbury*, which granted judges authority to decide only issues of law and directed them to avoid political decision making, differed significantly from judicial review as it is practiced today, when judges frequently make choices of policy. But, unlike Hobson, I am not concerned whether Marshall's decision in *Marbury* was consistent with classical, eighteenth-century political thought, while unlike Clinton, I am not concerned whether the decision was consistent with technical legal doctrines of the Blackstone era.

My main objective is neither to criticize nor to praise *Marbury v. Madison*. Rather, my goal is to assist readers in understanding the decision as a step in the ongoing elaboration of American and, more recently, global constitutionalism. In particular, I hope to establish something different from what other historians have shown—namely, how the Marshall Court, in deciding *Marbury*, was striving to preserve what the justices and nearly all their fellow citizens found best in eighteenth-century constitutionalism, while at the same time accommodating that constitutionalism to new nineteenth-century political realities. I also will attempt in the closing chapters of the book to explain how *Marbury*-style judicial review, which was grounded in a distinction between law and politics, was transformed over the next century and a half into today's judicial review, which we understand inevitably requires judges to resolve contentious issues of constitutional social policy.

Thus, my story begins with an analysis of the constitutional polity of eighteenth-century, colonial British North America. My central claim, however counterintuitive it may seem to Americans at the outset of the twenty-first century, is that mid-eighteenth-century British colonials did not want any government entity to engage in social policy choice. They understood law as fixed and immutable, not as something that government could change in response to shifting conceptions of social good. Indeed, they equated fixed law with liberty and changeable law with arbitrary rule and tyranny.

However, during the four decades between the end of the Seven Years War with France in 1763 and the decision of *Marbury v. Madison* in 1803, Americans engaged in debate with advocates of parliamentary sovereignty, declared their independence, fought a war to establish it, drafted and ratified a new constitution, and put a new government into operation. And, for the first time in American history, the election of 1800 peacefully transferred power from a political group advocating one set of social policies to a rival party advocating opposing policies. Thus, by 1803, the American public could not avoid recognition of the fact that law sometimes did change as a result of policy choice.

But their understanding that some legal change was inevitable did not mean that they found change desirable or that they expected significant amounts of change to continue to occur. Americans still understood that liberty was founded upon fixed and immutable laws, however much the democratic political process might debate policy choice and result in social change. The core thesis of this book is that in *Marbury v. Madison*, Chief Justice John Marshall drew a line, which nearly all citizens of his time believed ought to be drawn, between the legal and the political—between those matters on which all Americans agreed and which therefore were fixed and immutable and those matters which were subject to fluctuation and change through democratic politics.

The right to private property was on the legal side of the line. The vast majority of adult white men in early nineteenth-century America either already owned land or expected to acquire land at some point during their lives. Moreover, they understood that the law protected and should protect ownership rights. Although they also understood that the law regulated property rights, little demand existed for regulation of a redistributive nature. Thus, when the Marshall Court in *Marbury v. Madison* declared that rights akin to the right of property in land were immune from political regulation, virtually all Americans agreed that the Court's decision was correct.

For more than a century after *Marbury*, judges continued to protect private property, as they had always done. In doing so, they could understand that they were preserving the law of property as something fixed and immutable—that they were upholding Marshall's distinction between law and politics. But as vast accumulations of commercial wealth, which conferred monopoly power on their holders and enabled them to dominate others' lives, grew in the late nineteenth century, demands for redistributive regulation grew, and those who demanded the new regulation came to see the judiciary's protection of established rights as controversial and political rather than as legal and immutable. For some Americans, at least, Marshall's distinction between law and politics began to dissolve, and judicial review began to pass into the realm of policy choice.

The demand for redistributive regulation triumphed during the New Deal, and beginning in 1937, the New Dealers remade the Supreme Court. The Court, in turn, made the political choice to abandon its traditional protection of property rights and to enter upon a new role of safeguarding discrete and insular racial, religious, and cultural minorities who could not protect themselves through majoritarian democratic politics. This new role, in turn, involved the Court in *ad hoc* balancing of the policy claims put forth by minorities against the claims of legislative majorities.

Thus, judicial review as we know it today came to fruition. And, as Chapter 8 will show, it has spread throughout a world that never shared John Marshall's concern in *Marbury v. Madison* about how to distinguish law from politics, but that, like America at the outset of a new century, struggles continuously with the issue of reconciling the rights of ethnic, religious, and cultural minorities with the power of dominant political majorities.

CHAPTER I

The Consensual Community

The social structure of mid-eighteenth-century British North America differed profoundly from the social structure of the United States today. Eighteenth-century British colonials were more tied to their families and rooted in their localities than most Americans are today; they were not free-floating individuals, like many of us, who select the other individuals with whom we will form close relationships.

Nor did most eighteenth-century colonials determine in their youth what they would become as adults. Rather they were born into the economic, social, and cultural networks around which their adult lives typically would center. Most colonials were children of farmers and would themselves become farmers when they attained maturity. Few had the option, by choosing some profession other than farming, of becoming embedded in a network different from that into which they had been born. Although they might hope to prosper, to increase their wealth, and even to obtain more land, few could imagine, as many of us do, that they had the capacity either to change their lives or to change the world around them.

Family ties bound individuals to their neighborhood. Consider, for example, Elizabeth Montague of Middlesex County, Virginia, who at the time of her death was related by blood or marriage to three-fourths of the households in the county. Family connections such as those enjoyed by Montague provided an individual with invaluable support in times of crisis and stress, such as impoverishment, illness, violent onslaught, or even death in the immediate family. At a time when government, market, and charitable institutions such as police, hospitals, doctors, schools, and welfare agencies were weak or nonexistent, a person's ties to family were often the only means that could save her from standing helpless and alone in the wilderness in times of trouble. Family ties were so important that many people, especially families, elderly people, and single women, dared not leave a community where they had ties and move to one where they would dwell in isolation.

Family ties also had another impact: they deprived people of privacy and anonymity. In neighborhoods where everyone was known, there could be no secrets and no anonymous misbehavior. If a person broke the neighborhood's moral code or failed to perform a duty that the community required, gossip would promptly spread news of the breach or failure to everyone. A youth's parents, family, and neighbors, like the all-knowing God, learned of every one of his peccadilloes.

Societal realities such as these determined the scope and design of government. By the middle of the eighteenth century, eleven of the thirteen North American colonies had governors appointed by the crown or by proprietors in England, while only two, Connecticut and Rhode Island, had elected governors. But all these governors were weak and dependent on the other main institution of colonial government—the legislature, which possessed some important powers. Its most critical was the power of the purse. Only the legislature could vote to raise taxes needed to pay the governor's and other officials' salaries and to fund any special undertakings, such as wars, in which the governor or crown officials in London wished to engage. Legislatures often used their power to refuse to vote taxes as a bargaining chip to gain other concessions from governors.

Another important legislative power was the jurisdiction and obligation to create local institutions. Acts of the legislature, for example, created counties, which were the locus of governmental power throughout colonial British North America; identified the location of county seats; and, at least in some colonies, most notably Massachusetts, authorized families to establish churches.

Such legislation was enormously important to local residents. People in newly settled areas who were several hours distant from an established county obtained the ability to govern themselves and, indeed, the advantages of government itself, when the legislature established their locality as a new county. Landowners proximate to a location chosen as a county seat or other site of government profited from the influx of people seeking government services and accordingly worked hard to influence the legislature's choice. And the capacity to establish a local church and compel all families to contribute to its support gave a community access to religious solace, created a neighborhood social center, and furnished a locality with a learned mediator who could call on the power of the ministry to assist in the resolution of personal problems and conflicts.

On occasion, legislatures also enacted statutes of general applicability, such as a Virginia law of 1740 providing for the inspection, grading, and sealing of tobacco leaves and a Massachusetts law of 1761 providing the death penalty for convicted robbers and burglars. Indeed, in the seventeenth century, important legislation had created the institution of slavery. But by the eighteenth century, general laws were enacted only infrequently. One reason was that the general laws adopted by most colonial legislatures were subject to a complex process of review in England, where they could be and frequently were disallowed. A more important reason for the sparsity of legislation was that no one conceived of law as an instrument for social change. Indeed, no one had a clear conception of even the possibility of social change.

Thus, once they had been established, communities tended to become simply ongoing. Inactive legislatures and weak governors rarely interfered in local affairs. Even if they had wanted to interfere, they lacked any real capacity for doing so. Eighteenth-century government, unlike government today, did not consist of a ubiquitous bureaucracy with clear chains of command reaching upward to central political authorities. There were no police, state or local; no department of motor vehicles; no highway department; no state education bureaucracy. There was no colonial equivalent, on any level of government, to the Internal Revenue Service or the Social Security Administration.

Because there was no modern bureaucracy, the judiciary and the officials, such as sheriffs, responsible to it were the primary link between a colony's central government and its outlying localities. The judiciary alone could coerce individuals by punishing crimes and imposing money judgments. In some colonies, such as Massachusetts and Virginia, the judiciary was virtually the whole of local government, but even in colonies where other officials were available, those officials were subject to judicial control. As one member of Congress observed in an end-of-the-century recapitulation, "[o]ther departments of the Government" may have been "more splendid," but only the "courts of justice [came] home to every man's habitation."

The vital role of the courts in colonial government did not, however, mean that government performed only functions that we today would classify as judicial. Colonial government regulated its subjects' lives in pervasive detail. The courts, as a vital part of the government, maintained order, protected life and property, apportioned and collected taxes, supervised the construction and maintenance of highways, issued licenses, and regulated licensees' businesses. Through administration of the Settlement Law, which permitted localities to exclude undesired newcomers, and the Poor Law, which made localities liable for the support and hence the general well-being of all who were born and raised in a locality and all newcomers who were not excluded, the legal system fostered community self-definition and a sense of community responsibility for inhabitants. Indeed, in some colonies, the courts of general sessions of the peace, which possessed basic criminal and administrative jurisdiction and some minor forms of civil jurisdiction, also performed the executive and even the legislative functions of local government.

The work of the courts, in sum, was of an undifferentiated, pervasive character. The undifferentiated character of that work was important for present purposes because it obscured distinctions that political theorists draw between legislation, administration, and adjudication. Despite the early statement of Baron Montesquieu, the French theorist of the modern doctrine of separation of powers, Americans as late as the 1780s did not routinely distinguish the judiciary as an independent branch that exercised only "judicial" functions: they did not, that is, draw a clear distinction between law and politics. As one anonymous tract published in 1776 observed,

> Government is generally distinguished into three parts, Executive, Legislative and Judicial, but this is more a distinction of words than things. . . . [H]owever we may refine and define, there is no more than two powers in any government, viz, the power to make laws, and the power to execute them; for the judicial power is only a branch of the executive, the CHIEF of every country being the first magistrate.

Even though most British American colonials did not draw clear distinctions between the judiciary and other branches of government, they still did not understand that judges possessed policy-making prerogatives of the sort that we assume Congress and the president possess today. It was a commonplace, as Chief Justice Thomas Hutchinson of Massachusetts informed a grand jury in 1769, that those who "execut[ed] the Law . . . [ought] not to enquire into . . . [its] Reason and Policy," but ought merely "to enquire what is Law."

Daniel Dulaney, an early thinker from Maryland, agreed in 1728 that courts merely dispensed justice according to law, which was thought to be *"founded in principles, that are permanent*, uniform *and* universal." It was vital, as Hutchinson said in other grand jury charges in the late 1760s, that "the Laws of every State ought always to be fixed, [and] certain" and that *"the Judge* should never be the *Legislator:* Because, then the Will of the Judge would be the Law: and this tends to a State of Slavery." A young lawyer who would oppose Hutchinson in the War for Independence and ultimately would become the second president of the United States, John Adams, wrote at approximately the same time as Hutchinson was delivering his charges that "every possible Case" ought to be "settled in a Precedent leav[ing] nothing, or but little to the arbitrary Will or uninformed Reason of Prince or Judge."

The chief executive of each colony—the governor—similarly was thought to have no power to make policy. The same was true for the chief executive of the realm—the king—who by the mid-eighteenth century possessed little real power. Some colonials even had doubts about the power of the legislature to enact laws. For example, James Otis Jr., another Massachusetts opponent of the loyalist Hutchinson, argued during the 1760s that legislation "contrary to eternal truth, equity, and justice" would be void, since "the supreme power in a state . . . [was] *jus dicere* only . . . [, while] *jus dare*, strictly speaking, belong[ed] only to GOD." Thus, even before the late-eighteenth-century adoption of written constitutions, arguments were being made, in the words of a 1775 New York pamphlet, that "something must exist in a free state, which no part of it can be authorised to alter or destroy."

To understand how colonials held such views, we need to focus on what has already been mentioned above—that the eighteenth century was a time when few people imagined that social change was possible and nearly everyone assumed that life would go on essentially as it had for decades. Society was seen as a stable organism that grew and maintained itself of its own accord.

It followed from this view of society that no one in government needed to make choices about the direction that law, government, and the society ought to take. Of course, bad people might threaten the health and stability of the organism: foreign monarchs often threatened its destruction by war, and criminals and other evil people posed menaces to its peace and stability at home. The king had the duty to make the decisions needed to protect the realm from foreign threats, and his courts performed the task of doing justice to malefactors at home. But doing justice did not entail policy choice; it necessitated only the enforcement of traditional, customary values, such as property, stability, community, and morality, which were embedded deeply within existing common law.

It is also essential to emphasize that in doing justice courts did not coerce the good people of a community; on the contrary, they worked harmoniously with those people to protect and defend the embedded values that most people of the community took for granted. The judges who directed county and colony-wide courts were prominent local and colonial leaders, but they were leaders who had power only to guide, not to command. Juries rather than judges spoke the last word on law enforcement in nearly all, if not all, of the eighteenth-century American colonies.

A few of the original thirteen colonies possessed courts of equity, which were modeled on the Chancery Court of England and which, like it, sat without juries. These equity courts occasionally— though often with multiyear breaks between sittings—decided cases. Except in these courts of equity, however, colonial judges could not enter a judgment or impose any but the most trivial of penalties without a jury verdict. And eighteenth-century American juries, unlike juries today, usually possessed the power to find both law and fact in the cases in which they sat.

In American courts of today, judges give juries charges or instructions on the law, and if a jury fails to follow the instructions, its verdict, except for a verdict acquitting a defendant charged with a crime, will be set aside. Eighteenth-century American judges, in contrast, often did not give clear instructions on the law, and even when they did, they lacked procedural mechanisms for compelling juries to follow them.

Instructions to juries lacked clarity for several reasons. First, it appears that in many cases instructions were brief and rudimentary. In Massachusetts, for example, lawyers could and did assume, as did James Sullivan, a future governor of the state, in a 1779 letter to Elbridge Gerry, another future governor, that jurors were "good judges of the common law of the land." John Adams had agreed in one of his pre-Revolutionary cases that "[t]he general Rules of Law and common Regulations of Society, under which ordinary Transactions arrange[d] themselves . . . [were] well enough known to ordinary Jurors." Accordingly, juries might be directed, as one superior court judge in fact directed them in 1759, that, as to many matters, they "need[ed] no Explanation [since] your Good Sence & understanding will Direct ye as to them."

In Connecticut, as a general practice, courts merely summarized the opposing claims without commenting on the law involved in pending cases, while in New Hampshire one judge told a jury "to do justice between the parties not by any quirks of the law . . . but by common sense as between man and man." Likewise, in one 1707 criminal case in colonial New York, the chief justice informed the jury that "there are some points [of law] I am not now prepared to answer," while in another 1741 case the court charged the jury only that the evidence from the prosecution's witnesses seemed "so ample, so full, so clear and satisfactory" that it should convict the prisoner "if you have no particular reasons in your own breast, in your consciences to discredit them."

Similarly, in South Carolina civil litigation in the 1780s, one jury was instructed "to find a general verdict, or a special one, . . . as they thought proper," while another jury was told "to give what they thought reasonable" in "damages." In other cases, no instructions were given at all. In Virginia, for example, according to one commentator who reviewed eighteenth-century practice in an 1831 brief, there were "numerous cases" in which the jury "retired without a word said by the court upon the subject" of the case.

Instructions were also ineffective because they were often contradictory. One potential source of contradiction was counsel, who on summation could argue the law as well as the facts. Most confusing of all was the court's charge. Nearly every court in eighteenth-century America sat with more than one judge on the bench, and it appears to have been the general rule for every judge who was sitting to deliver a charge if he wished to do so. Sometimes, judges were not unanimous. In both Massachusetts and South Carolina there are examples from the Revolutionary period of judges giving conflicting instructions to juries, and as late as 1803 Alexander Addison, a common pleas judge in Pennsylvania, was successfully impeached for refusing to permit other judges on his court to address juries.

Of course, whenever jurors received conflicting instructions, they were left with power to determine which judge's interpretation of the law and the facts was correct. Even when the court's instructions were unanimous, however, juries could not be compelled to adhere to them. Once jurors had received evidence on several factual issues and on the parties' possibly conflicting interpretations of the law, a court could compel them to decide in accordance with its view of the case only by setting aside any verdict contrary either to its statement of the law or to the evidence. By the 1750s English courts, upon motion of the losing party, would set aside such a verdict and order a new trial, but eighteenth-century American jurisdictions did not follow English practice.

Indeed, the English approach was not even considered except in the 1763 New York case of *Forsey v. Cunningham*, where three judges declared in letters written after the conclusion of the case that they had power to set aside jury verdicts contrary to the judges' instructions or to the evidence. But during the course of the case itself, the court in fact refused to grant a motion to set aside the verdict. Thus, it appears that the procedural mechanisms for constraining jury freedom to determine the law, which were developed in mid-eighteenth-century England, were never used during that period in America and that American juries thus were free to ignore instructions from judges on the law.

It accordingly seems safe to conclude that juries in most, if not all, eighteenth-century American jurisdictions normally had the power to determine law as well as fact in both civil and criminal cases. Statements of contemporary lawyers, moreover, buttress this conclusion: Zephaniah Swift, a Connecticut lawyer and judge, wrote in the mid-1790s, for instance, that "[t]he jury were the proper judges, not only of the fact but of the law that was necessarily involved" in each case, while Robert Treat Paine, a Massachusetts attorney, had argued to juries in the late 1760s and early 1770s that the "Jury ha[d] a right to do as they please[d]" and that "no verdicts . . . [were] thrown out."

Even more telling, perhaps, are statements by three of the most eminent lawyers in late eighteenth-century America—John Adams, Thomas Jefferson, and John Jay. In the early 1770s, Adams observed in his diary: "It was never yet disputed, or doubted, that a general Verdict, given *under the Direction of the Court* in Point of Law, was a legal Determination of the Issue." Adams argued that even a verdict contrary to the court's directions should stand, for it was "not only . . . [every juror's] right but his Duty in that Case to find the Verdict according to his own best Understanding, Judgment and Conscience, tho in Direct opposition to the Direction of the Court."

In 1781–1782, Thomas Jefferson painted an equally broad picture of the power of juries over the law in his *Notes on Virginia*. "It is usual for the jurors to decide the fact, and to refer the law arising on it to the decision of the judges," Jefferson wrote. "But this division of the subject lies with their discretion only. And if the question relate to any point of public liberty, or if it be one of those in which the judges may be suspected of bias, the jury undertake to decide both law and fact." And, as late as 1793, John Jay, sitting as chief justice of the United States, informed a civil jury that it had "a right to take upon yourselves to judge of both, and to determine the law as well as the fact in controversy." "[B]oth objects," Jay concluded, "are lawfully, within your power of decision."

The power of juries to determine law as well as fact reveals a great deal about government and society in eighteenth-century America. First, it reveals the communitarian locus of power and the weakness of central government authorities. Consider, for example, the 1761 Massachusetts case of *Erving v. Cradock*, in which a shipowner brought a writ of trespass against a royal revenue officer who had seized his vessel on a charge of smuggling and obtained a judgment in a royal vice-admiralty court, which decreed the vessel and its cargo forfeited to the crown. All five judges of the colony's highest court were convinced that the admiralty decree constituted a final disposition of the case and thus was a bar to the common law trespass suit, and they so instructed the jury. Yet when the jury ignored their instructions, returned a verdict for the shipowner, and, as a practical matter, thereby reversed the admiralty decree, the judges did not set the verdict aside and grant a new trial, although they fully realized that such verdicts nullified enforcement of the Navigation Acts in Massachusetts.

Why, it might be asked, did the judges so abdicate to the jury responsibility for deciding whether the Navigation Acts could be enforced in Massachusetts? The answer, in large part, is that the judges lacked power to do otherwise. Although the judges of the common law courts were appointed by the governor and their commissions ran only during the governor's pleasure, no Massachusetts judge was removed from office by the governor during the period from 1760 to 1774. Once appointed, judges were quite free from the influence of the crown. In contrast, their freedom from the lower house of the legislature, collectively the representative of the towns, was much more in doubt. Their salaries were under legislative control, and when it appeared likely in the 1770s that the crown would undertake to pay those salaries, the legislature threatened to impeach judges who accepted such payments.

Judges' susceptibility to local pressures was heightened throughout the thirteen colonies by the fact that nearly all judges were not drawn from the lower reaches of the English bureaucracy, but rather were men of local prominence. The key to becoming a judge was not that one was a lawyer, for nearly all colonial judges were not, but that one was a man of substance who commanded the respect of his community. Men who had obtained place in part because they possessed the trust and confidence of their fellow subjects would not lightly violate that trust. Although they were appointed by the crown, judges usually sought to retain the confidence and respect of their local communities and hence would be unlikely to reject legal traditions, such as those concerning the power of juries, that were widely esteemed in their community.

Even if judges had been inclined to ignore precedent and to overrule jury decisions on questions of law, it is doubtful whether they could have enforced their judgments. The crucial fact about government in mid-eighteenth-century America was that subordinate officials such as sheriffs, deputy sheriffs, and constables—the men with legal responsibility for enforcing judgments—could do so only when local communities were willing to permit judgments to be enforced. The difficulty was not merely that subordinate officials were liable to suits for damages, for that liability could have been judicially limited. A greater difficulty lay in the Anglo-American tradition of government—a tradition with roots in the Middle Ages and still very much alive in the eighteenth-century English world. In that tradition, government did not have vast bureaucratic armies of officials to enforce its laws, but instead relied on its subjects to aid the few officials who did exist in their task of law enforcement.

{ *Marbury v. Madison* }

The ultimate difficulty was that officials simply lacked effective power to coerce people to obey the law. Coercive use of violence by government simply could not bring victory in eighteenth-century America over recalcitrant individuals who had supporters in their community. If an official failed by himself to coerce a recalcitrant person, he could not call for the aid of a substantial body of force other than fellow members of the community, organized as the militia; if the militia was on the side of the recalcitrant person, it would not, of course, aid the official. Thus, the only way for officials to ensure enforcement of the law was to obtain local community support for the law, and the best way to obtain that support was to permit local communities to determine the substance of the law through legal institutions such as the jury.

The second reality that the law-making power of juries reveals is the fixed and certain nature of the law. If law had been uncertain and individual jurors had manifested differing opinions about its substance, it would have been impossible for jurors to have decided cases after receiving rudimentary or conflicting instructions, or even no instructions at all. The law-finding power of juries suggests ineluctably that jurors came to court with shared preconceptions about the substance of the law.

This point was explicitly made in the 1788 Connecticut case of *Pettis v. Warren*. In a black slave's suit for freedom, one juror was challenged for having a preexisting opinion "'that no negro, by the laws of this state, could be holden a slave.'" Affirming the trial court's overruling of the challenge, the Connecticut Supreme Court held that "[a]n opinion formed and declared upon a general principle of law, does not disqualify a juror to sit in a cause in which that principle applies." Indeed, the court observed that the jurors in every case could "all be challenged on one side or the other, if having an opinion of the law in the case is ground of challenge," since, as John Adams had noted some two decades earlier, "[t]he general Rules of Law and common Regulations of Society . . . [were] well enough known to ordinary Jurors." Jurors, the Connecticut court believed, were "supposed to have opinions of what the law is," since they sat as "judges of law as well as fact."

One might infer further that jurors came to the court with

similar preconceptions about the law, at least as it applied to disputes that frequently came before them. Indeed, one cannot escape this inference without abandoning all efforts to understand how eighteenth-century government functioned. If jurors came to court with different and possibly conflicting opinions about substantive law, one would expect to find first, that juries had difficulty reaching unanimous verdicts and that mistrials due to hung juries were correspondingly frequent, and second, that different juries at different times would reach different, perhaps inconsistent, verdicts, thereby making the law so uncertain and unpredictable that people could not plan their affairs.

In fact, no such evidence exists. On the contrary, the available evidence suggests that juries had so little difficulty reaching verdicts that they often heard and decided several cases a day. No one in the mid-eighteenth century complained about the inconsistency of jury verdicts, and as soon as such complaints were heard in the century's last decade, the system of jury law finding began to disintegrate.

Although we have no direct evidence, most subjects probably did not desire to serve as jurors. At a time of difficult travel, few people would have cared to attend court sessions, and those who did probably were pursuing business interests from which jury duty was an unwelcome distraction. In short, there is every reason to think that eighteenth-century subjects avoided jury duty as eagerly as citizens today and that the chore was therefore distributed among as much of the eligible population as could be conscripted. Although some groups (notably women, blacks, servants, religious dissenters, and anyone who did not own land or pay taxes) may have been systematically excluded from juries, it does not seem unreasonable to infer that juries contained a random and representative cross section of the remaining population.

That conclusion suggests a final inference. If juries in fact mirrored the white, male, landholding, and taxpaying population, and if upon coming to court nearly all jurors shared similar ideas about the substance of the law, then perhaps a body of shared ideas about law permeated a large segment of the population of every territory over which a court that sat with a jury had jurisdiction. Colonial government may have been able to derive policies from and otherwise function on the basis of those shared values.

Those who have lived amidst the twentieth-century cacophony of conflicting interests may find it difficult to imagine how a government acting only in the absence of serious conflict could ever function effectively. The eighteenth-century Anglo-American world, however, was sufficiently different from our own so that government in that era might have so functioned.

Several differences should be noted. First, the colonial economy was much less productive than is the economy today. As a result, less money was available for government, and most communities could afford only a few salaried officeholders. Indeed, many people did not have enough wealth and time even to participate in elections "without manifest injury to their crops."

Competition for local leadership positions also was understandably slight, and local governments lacked substantial salaried bureaucracies that could enforce decisions. Part-time police officials such as deputy sheriffs and constables enforced government decisions—so long, that is, as they did not contravene the wishes of neighbors with whom they had close economic and social ties. The ultimate enforcement body, the militia, was merely the community itself organized as a quasi-military body that would, of course, not act against the community's wishes. Colonial economic conditions, in short, reduced conflict and competition in local politics and precluded the rise of coercive institutions that might have been used by one portion of a community seeking to promote its interests at the expense of others.

Second, colonial American communities differed tremendously. Religion remained important in eighteenth-century life, and America provided room for many different religious groups. Religious differences were not the only ones among the communities. Important economic differences also existed, for while most communities were agricultural, a few either were mercantile or chiefly engaged in fishing. Finally, inarticulable differences in lifestyle and ambience distinguished communities, as any visitor of the restored colonial towns of Sturbridge, Massachusetts, and Williamsburg, Virginia, can see, or as any reader of the diaries of eighteenth-century travelers like Dr. Alexander Hamilton can learn.

Men who found it important to change their residence from one community to another were able to do so. Benjamin Franklin, the foremost American of the mid-eighteenth century, had moved in his youth from Boston to Philadelphia with relative ease, for instance, while thousands of colonial Americans found the move from established towns to the frontier not at all insuperable. As a result, most colonials who dissented from their own community's conception of right and justice could move without great difficulty to a more congenial community. Newly arriving immigrants were also able to identify and settle in communities that welcomed their religious beliefs, lifestyles, and economic skills. The tendency of people to live in communities they found congenial was important, particularly because it enabled communities to retain their identity by facilitating the departure of those whose personal ethical codes would have diluted that identity.

But while colonial Americans could readily move between communities, they generally seem not to have established the kind of sustained intercommunity contact likely to produce conflict. American communities had long since abandoned schemes of subjugating each other or seizing each other's wealth; the Dutch of Manhattan and the Puritans of Long Island, for example, learned how to coexist when they each abandoned thoughts of conquest and developed their primary social and economic communication with their respective compatriots in the Hudson Valley and in New England rather than with each other. The availability of land, which made territorial quarrels unnecessary, and the lack of a developed transportation and communication network, which made sustained contact difficult, also help account for the infrequency of disputes between communities. Geographically proximate communities were thus able to remain distinct, to pursue their own conception of right, and to avoid intercommunity disputes that legal institutions dependent on local community support would have been incapable of resolving.

Finally, colonial politics existed within an established constitutional structure, which colonials could not control. Parliament, in which colonials had no direct voice, alone possessed the power to decide many fundamental social and economic issues, and for the first sixty years of the eighteenth century it was willing to abide by decisions reached in the preceding century, which were often favorable to the colonies. Thus, much of the grist for genuine political conflict was removed from the realm of imperial politics; absent a radical restructuring of the Anglo-American system, there was simply no point in building a political organization around the issue, for example, whether Anglicans would be tolerated in Massachusetts or whether Americans would be free to trade with French Canada without restriction.

Provincial politics were not radically different. Colonial legislatures were under American control, but they could not effectively enact legislation that significantly altered the structure of colonial society since such legislation would almost always be vetoed by a colonial governor or by London. As a result, colonial legislation usually consisted of mere administration: raising and appropriating small amounts of tax money, distributing the even smaller amounts of government largess, and legislating as necessary to keep the few governmental institutions functioning.

While provincial political conflict commonly occurred, it rarely involved important social issues. Of course, occasional conflicts grew from religious differences, such as the division in Pennsylvania politics between Quaker and anti-Quaker parties, and from the rivalry between seaboard and backcountry areas, such as the 1740s land-bank dispute in Massachusetts and the 1760s Regulator Movement in the Carolinas. But since these disputes could not be locally resolved within the British power structure, they quickly degenerated into mere personal and factional conflicts between leaders seeking personal advancement. Provincial political conflict may have been widespread, but as shrewdly observant colonial political writers vehemently announced, it departed from the ideal polity of consensus—a polity that may have existed in many eighteenth-century local communities.

Taken together, these facts helped to sustain a political order in colonial America radically different from the political order of America today. The stable imperial constitution combined with the penury of colonial economies to remove most social and economic issues from imperial and provincial politics. Before independence, most newly arising socioeconomic conflicts were resolved and new socioeconomic decisions taken at the local level.

The penury of colonial economies had another influence: by keeping the social elite small and depriving it of effective military and bureaucratic power necessary to coerce the people at large, the political economy of British North America denied colonial leaders the opportunity to exploit their localities in their own self-interest. Leaders generally had to govern and resolve social tensions according to values widely accepted in their localities. Finally, the real differences between localities and the ease with which men could move to a community whose ideas they shared preserved each community's distinct identity.

As a result, the colonial American polity may, on the whole, have consisted of a series of local communities whose inhabitants collectively strove to define standards of right and justice and to govern their communities by those standards. Of course, they did not always succeed. As many historians have shown, a communitarian social order had at least partially broken down by the time of the American Revolution, when social conflict and tension had become endemic. Perhaps the breakdown even contributed to the Revolution. Moreover, many people—notably, African-American slaves, Native Americans, women, and landless white men—were not even part of the political community, and tensions between them and the landowning white males who did constitute the community were ever present. Historians also have pointed to a good deal of conflict within the white, male, landowning community.

Nonetheless, the structure of colonial government was such that it could function effectively only in jurisdictions with some degree of consensus and shared values. When societal conflict escalated, colonial government became ineffective, as it did in many places during the decade leading up to the Revolution. Government broke down and violent conflict ensued with some frequency in the second half of the eighteenth century precisely because government had few mechanisms other than the building of consensus with which to obtain obedience to its mandates. Government based upon shared values may have functioned in eighteenth-century America with only a minimal degree of effectiveness, but no other style of government was capable of functioning at all.

With this, we come to the most important point for purposes of this book. The point is that a consensus style of government was known to most mid-eighteenth-century white, male Americans on a routine, day-to-day basis. An individual litigant, a special-interest group, a high provincial official, even a judge, often could elicit a particular court decision or attain a long-term policy only if he could persuade the cross section of the community that acted as jurors, and such attempts at persuasion must almost invariably have required appeals to values he and the jurors shared. Since eighteenth-century juries rarely could be circumvented or coerced, there was normally no other way to proceed.

Of course, lawyers, judges, officials, and litigants did not always find common values that could support decisions. They may often have failed, and their failures may have sensitized them to the instability inherent in processes of government by consensus. Nevertheless, the mid-eighteenth-century statesman typically was compelled to govern, the lawyer was required to practice, and the litigant was forced to argue, by molding and appealing to a consensus of shared values. It was in this style of government and legal practice that John Marshall, the author of *Marbury v. Madison*, and other statesmen, judges, and lawyers of his generation first learned their professions.

CHAPTER 2

The Politics of Constitutional Change

We saw in Chapter 1 how the routine, day-by-day practices of governance in mid-eighteenth-century America depended to some significant degree on the existence of an established Anglo-American constitutional structure, which colonials could neither alter nor control. In this chapter, we shall examine how, after the end in 1763 of the Seven Years War, known in America as the French and Indian War, that structure became unhinged.

The war transformed the imperial structure in two profound respects. For the first six decades of the eighteenth century, French control of Canada, the Great Lakes, and the entire Mississippi basin had placed the western boundary of the British North American colonies at the crest of the Appalachian range, which runs through northern New England, central New York and Pennsylvania, and western Virginia and North Carolina. The French and their Indian allies had inhibited land-hungry American colonials from even contemplating the establishment of agricultural settlements on the western side of the Appalachians. But when a British army captured Quebec in 1760 and occupied Montreal the next year, French power was doomed. By the 1763 treaty ending the war, France transferred the city of New Orleans and all of the Mississippi basin west of the Mississippi River to Spain. France ceded the remainder of its territory on the North American continent to Great Britain.

With the elimination of French power from North America, land speculators and prospective settlers could hope that settlement of the trans-Appalachian West would be encouraged. Their hopes were set back, however, when the ministry in London issued the Proclamation of 1763, which limited settlement to lands east of the crest of the Appalachians. But the possibility of trans-Appalachian settlement did not go away. French and Indian opposition to settlement could remove its possibility from the political and social agenda of British North Americans, but London's opposition could not. Americans regarded the Proclamation of 1763 as a grievance throughout the remainder of the colonial era, and a few of them even challenged London's capacity to enforce the Proclamation by ignoring it and establishing homes and farms west of the Proclamation line.

The second significant impact of the Seven Years War was on the British government's budget. Great Britain had incurred enormous financial costs during the war, which had created a burgeoning national debt. The war also left Great Britain with rising expenditures resulting from increased military obligations in newly acquired territories such as Canada. The result was increasing debt service and rising taxes. When the ministry in London looked for new sources of revenue to cover its growing fiscal needs, it came to the judgment that its North American colonies, which were among the principal beneficiaries of the war, ought to be taxed to pay for its costs. Parliament agreed and enthusiastically passed the Sugar Act of 1764 and then the Stamp Act of 1765.

America was never again the same. Colonial leaders organized widespread resistance to parliamentary taxation, and they succeeded in procuring the repeal of both the Sugar Act and the Stamp Act. But Parliament insisted upon its power to tax in the Declaratory Act of 1766, which proclaimed Parliament's sovereign power to legislate for its North American colonies in all cases whatsoever, and in subsequent years it periodically imposed limited taxes. Meanwhile, the colonials, who had learned how to mount continent-wide resistance during the Stamp Act crisis, maintained their opposition to Parliament's sovereignty claim.

This is not the place to analyze the vast historical literature on the pre-Revolutionary constitutional conflict nor to discuss, in any detail, the conflict itself. It will suffice to note that violent rebellion broke out in April of 1775 at Lexington and Concord. A year later, on July 4, 1776, the Declaration of Independence was adopted, and the thirteen colonies of British North America became the free and independent United States.

At the outset of the War of Independence, most rebelling colonists aimed not so much to change as to preserve the basic structure of the political system under which they had lived prior to what they viewed as Parliament's attempts to subvert it between 1763 and 1775. In particular, most Americans wished to preserve a political order that generally required officials to govern according to common, shared values or principles that nearly all citizens accepted as right or otherwise legitimate.

Nevertheless, independence significantly reshaped American politics by introducing a new political style that was in stark contrast to the mid-eighteenth-century style of government by consensus. Over the course of the next several years, the Continental Congress had to raise and support an army, appoint commanding generals, negotiate with foreign powers, and strive to place national power on a firm constitutional footing. Connected with this final task was the governance of the vast territories in the trans-Appalachian West that the United States would acquire from Great Britain in the 1783 peace treaty acknowledging American independence. In performing these tasks, Congress and other national officials had to make choices among possible policies that were in conflict with each other—choices that favored some American interests over others and thus could not be made on the basis of principles or values with which nearly everyone agreed.

These national issues impacted local politics. Most significant of all were the divisions in local communities resulting from the Revolutionary struggle itself, as citizens who identified themselves as patriots came into conflict with loyalists, those who remained committed to the cause of Parliament and the Crown. These conflicts sundered communities and often resulted in the exile of loyalists and the confiscation of their properties.

With the ratification of the Articles of Confederation, a new Confederation Congress came into being in 1781. But national political issues did not go away, nor did they cease to have an impact on local communities. Several issues growing out of the War of Independence and the 1783 peace accord were of special importance.

In order to obtain peace and independence and to secure British evacuation of all outposts in the newly recognized American territories, Congress had agreed in the 1783 treaty that individual British creditors would suffer no impediments to the collection of debts owed to them by Americans. But several states refused to honor this provision in the treaty and placed various impediments in the path of British creditors. Prospective lenders in Great Britain, knowing they would face future impediments as creditors, responded by tightening credit, while the British government reacted by refusing to evacuate outposts in the western portions of the new United States that the 1783 treaty had obligated it to surrender. As a result, Americans seeking to borrow money found it more difficult and expensive to do so, and those seeking to settle or otherwise exploit the West found the British army and its Indian allies in their path.

These actions by several American states, by British lenders, and by the British government created political divisions in local American communities that would endure into the early nineteenth century. On the one side were established farmers who had borrowed money in the past and now found repayment difficult or undesirable; they did not want Congress to interfere with state policies that made debt collection more difficult and created a possibility that they might avoid full repayment of their debts. Pitted against them were pioneers who found the British blocking their westward movement and business entrepreneurs seeking to borrow funds to expand their operations; they wanted a stronger national Congress that could compel the states to obey the peace treaty and otherwise advance their interests in westward expansion or international commerce. Clashes between these groups reverberated on the local, state, and national levels.

Above all, independence destroyed the constitutional order that had existed for a century in the British North American world. No longer were fundamental questions such as the distribution of power among various levels of government, the continuance of religious establishments, and the freedom of American merchants to trade abroad resolved by an imperial law that the colonies had little direct power to control. Independence compelled Americans to resolve such questions anew, often on a national rather than a local basis. Independence meant that newly independent Americans, unlike their colonial ancestors, would routinely need to make choices among competing policies and, as a result of those choices, structure the world in which they wanted to live. The post-Revolutionary generation's grapplings with these questions portended social discord in both state and national politics and during the last two decades of the eighteenth century provoked some of the most vituperative conflict that has ever occurred in American political history.

The revolutionary struggle and the attainment of independence also transformed American society and politics ideologically. In discarding British rule and reconstituting their governments, Americans proclaimed that all law springs from popular will as codified in legislation. If the people could remake their government, it followed, the *Maryland Journal* declared in 1787, that the lawmaking power of the people must be "original, inherent, and unlimited by human authority." A preacher who spoke to the Massachusetts legislature in 1782 identified popular will as "the only rational source of power," while in the next year the *Connecticut Courant* wrote that there was "an original, underived and incommunicable authority and supremacy in the collective body of the people to whom all delegated power must submit and from whom there is no appeal."

This concept of legislation as the creation of new law by the people or their representatives proved practically significant after independence because groups such as religious dissenters and westward expansionists used it to promote their interests. Before the Revolution, as we have seen, policies imposed by London had tended to restrict westward expansion and to require that dissenters support established churches. Once independent Americans could formulate their own policies, however, both religious dissenters and westward expansionists campaigned to revise established policies. Legislatures frequently responded by changing inherited rules and practices, and in the process changed themselves as well. By enacting new law, legislatures reinforced the ideology of popular lawmaking power and forged an active, creative legislative process in lieu of one that had depended on the derivation of rules from preexisting shared principles.

This transformation occurred, however, in a society unprepared to abandon blithely the pre-Revolutionary ideal that human law must conform to fundamental principles of divine or natural law. The older ideal persisted throughout the late 1770s and the 1780s.

Post-Revolutionary Americans continued to maintain, in the words of one Fourth of July speaker in Savannah, Georgia, in 1788, that they could rationally "define the rights of nature" and learn "how to search into, to distinguish, and to comprehend, the principles of physical, moral, religious, and civil liberty." Believing, as did Alexander Hamilton, an eminent attorney in the 1780s and later secretary of the treasury, in "eternal principles of social justice," the residents of Salem, New Jersey, in the mid-1780s, similarly objected to legislation "founded not upon the principles of Justice, but upon the Right of the Sword" and for which "no other Reason [could] be given . . . than because the Legislature had the Power and Will to enact such a Law." According to yet another 1786 article, this one in the *Providence Gazette*, legislators who enacted laws that "violate[d] . . . fundamental principles . . . [were] substituting *power* for *right*." A final thinker with a similar viewpoint was future president James Madison, who, arguing at the time of the Constitutional Convention for a congressional power to negate state legislation, noted in a letter to George Washington, the Revolutionary commander-in-chief who would soon become president, that America needed "some disinterested & dispassionate umpire" to control "disputes between different passions & interests in the State[s]."

In short, many Americans, even after the Revolution, continued to believe that government should articulate and apply fundamental principles dispassionately, neutrally, and objectively, rather than yield to a mere electoral majority. Some, like Madison, thought that legislatures, not courts, should guard fundamental legal principles, while others, like Hamilton, argued that courts as well as legislatures should do so. But since courts throughout the 1780s were still generally considered an undifferentiated segment of the executive branch, the important issue for that decade was not whether the legislative, executive, or judicial branch should ensure the conformity of law to fundamental standards of right, but whether any institution should.

At times during that decade, legislatures received criticism for failing to protect those fundamental standards. Arguments were made, for instance, at the Virginia convention that ratified the federal Constitution, against a Virginia act that had condemned to death an alleged highway robber "without any proof better than vague reports . . . [,] without being confronted with his accusers and witnesses, [and] without the privilege of calling for evidence in his behalf." To those who believed that law must adhere to immutable principles that transcend popular will, "this arbitrary deprivation of life, the dearest gift of God to man," was neither "consistent with the genius of republican government" nor "compatible with the spirit of freedom"; they could "not contemplate it without horror" and hoped that the new Constitution would render invalid any legislation contrary to fundamental principles.

But others took a different view. One leading intellectual, Noah Webster, argued in 1787 that the collective body of the people possessed "plenary power" to make law and that if the people were to be granted an "unlimited power to do *right*," then they must also be granted "an unlimited power to do *wrong*." Authorizing any group to nullify acts of the people, according to a North Carolina delegate at the 1787 federal Constitutional Convention, "would be more despotic than the Roman Decemvirate," for who could then "check or control" the nullifiers?

At still other times during the 1780s state courts heard demands for the protection of fundamental rights—demands that can be traced back to the decision of Chief Justice Edward Coke in *Bonham's Case* in 1610. This case had arisen when the Royal College of Physicians, on which Parliament had conferred exclusive power to govern the practice of medicine in London, prosecuted Dr. Bonham, adjudged him to be in violation of its rules,

{ *Marbury v. Madison* }

and then fined and imprisoned him. When Bonham brought a suit for false imprisonment, Coke decided in his favor on the ground that, in both prosecuting and adjudicating Bonham's case, the College of Physicians had violated the common law maxim that a man may not be judge in his own case. To the College's rejoinder that Parliament had authorized it to be both prosecutor and judge, Coke proclaimed the following dictum:

> And it appears in our books that in many cases the common law will controul acts of Parliament and sometimes adjudge them to be utterly void: for when an act of Parliament is against common right or reason, or repugnant, or impossible to be performed, the common law will controul it and adjudge such an act to be void.

On its face, Coke's dictum is ambiguous: it is not clear whether he invalidated the parliamentary statute because it violated what he called "common right"—an approach that would be akin to judicial review, which voids legislation that is inconsistent with fundamental constitutional principles, or whether he refused to apply the statute in the manner requested by the College of Physicians because it was repugnant or incapable of being performed consistently with its own terms—an approach that would be akin to statutory construction, where judges try to make sense out of ambiguous, possibly even inconsistent, legislation by interpreting it in light of established background common law principles. Judges inevitably must engage in the task of statutory construction, since legislative acts will always contain some ambiguity, and statutory construction does not threaten legislative supremacy, because a legislature can always overrule a court's constructional decision by reenacting its statute in unambiguous terms.

English cases in the century and a half after *Bonham's Case* increasingly read it as a statutory construction case, and Blackstone, in his *Commentaries on the Laws of England,* written in the 1760s, left no doubt that Parliament was supreme and that judges could not invalidate or otherwise refuse to apply legislation that they found contrary to common right. But, as we have seen, Americans in the 1760s were unwilling to accept Parliamentary supremacy, and this unwillingness gave rise to an important argument by a young Massachusetts lawyer, James Otis Jr., in the 1761 case of *Paxton v. Gray*.

The issue was whether the Superior Court of Massachusetts, as an act of Parliament authorized it to do, should issue writs of assistance to customs officers—writs that authorized the officers to enforce the customs laws that Parliament had enacted. Otis, who believed that customs searches violated the rights of the people of Massachusetts, offered diverse arguments about why the act of Parliament authorizing writs should not be applied. Among his arguments was a citation to *Bonham's Case*, together with a pronouncement that was later summarized by John Adams as follows:

> As to Acts of Parliament, An Act against the Constitution is void: An Act against natural Equity is void: and if the Act of Parliament should be made, in the very words of the Petition, it should be void. The . . . Courts must pass such Acts into disuse.

Otis's pronouncement was repeated with growing frequency during the course of the pre-Revolutionary debates with Great Britain, and indeed, was republished as late as 1773 in a Boston newspaper.

The *Writs of Assistance Case*, as *Paxton v. Gray* came to be known, and through it *Bonham's Case*, remained very much in the air in the aftermath of the War for Independence. Although not without their ambiguities, the two cases appeared at least to some American lawyers in the 1780s as a clarion call for judicial review and a clear challenge to the then dominant doctrine of legislative supremacy. They undoubtedly helped to spawn a series of state-court cases in the 1780s, in which claims akin to modern requests for judicial review were advanced.

On the whole, state courts treated the requests sympathetically. In four reported cases from North Carolina, Rhode Island, and Virginia, courts explicitly asserted the power to invalidate unconstitutional legislation; in two other cases from New York and South Carolina, they effectively struck down statutes under the guise of interpretation. Massachusetts and New Hampshire courts also held legislative acts unconstitutional in unreported cases. Well into the 1790s, state courts continued to hold state legislative acts unconstitutional, and in two cases during that decade, reported as *Hayburn's Case* and *Hylton v. United States,* the justices of the United States Supreme Court assumed—without, however, deciding the issue—that they too possessed power in an appropriate case to declare congressional legislation unconstitutional.

In many of these cases, advocates of the people's transcendent power to make law in their legislatures debated adherents of older notions of the inherent rightness and immutability of law. In the New York case, *Rutgers v. Waddington,* for example, the "supremacy of the Legislature . . . *positively* to enact a law" was pitted against "the rights of human nature" and the "law of nature." Similarly, in *Trevett v. Weeden* a Rhode Island act that penalized without jury trial anyone who refused to accept the state's paper currency was challenged as "contrary to the laws of nature" and violative of the "fundamental right" of "trial by jury."

But, as late as the early 1790s, the line between believers in popular sovereignty and believers in supreme fixed principles was rarely so plainly drawn. One could still believe simultaneously in the people's power to make law and in the immutability of the principles underlying law. Although it appreciated and accepted popular lawmaking, the Revolutionary generation did not abandon older notions that law made by the people must not violate rights that Americans had proclaimed immutably theirs in the struggle with England. New and old ideas coexisted as the Revolutionary generation, believing in the people's inherent goodness, simply assumed that all laws made by the people would be consistent with fundamental rights.

As the 1790s progressed, however, this ambivalent legal ideology proved merely transitory and diverged into two clearer, more coherent points of view. One sought to resolve all issues according to the will of the people, while the other sought to resolve them according to fixed principles of law. The appearance of these competing ideologies was closely related to the division in American politics in the 1790s between Federalists, who generally viewed law as a reflection of fixed and transcendent principles, and Republicans, who considered it the embodiment of popular will.

Future Federalists and Republicans first divided over the seemingly trivial issue of the chief executive's title—a matter that raised specters of monarchism. Even more divisive was the economic program of Secretary of the Treasury Alexander Hamilton. His plans to fund the national debt, which would require higher taxes, and to create a national bank, which portended tighter credit, stirred a more significant controversy. However, historians generally agree that the first truly national political organizations arose in the mid-1790s in response to the French Revolution and the signing of Jay's Treaty with Great Britain. These two events forced Americans to choose sides in the worldwide struggle between Britain and France that began in 1793, and for many the choice posed difficult ideological issues. Some Americans found themselves horrified by the excesses of the French Revolution during the early 1790s and by its culmination in the politically driven executions of the Reign of Terror; others, while not approving of the death and violence, remained convinced that the French republican movement would ultimately warrant American sympathy. Similarly, some thought that John Jay paid too high a price for British withdrawal from the Northwest Territory when he agreed in his treaty to have the federal government, in return, pay Revolutionary era debts still owed to British creditors.

The political divisions of the mid-1790s reflected ideological concerns as well. For example, the Federalists saw in Jefferson and the Republicans many of the threats to religion, to life, and to property that they found so horrifying in French revolutionaries. The election of 1800, according to one Federalist campaign tract, would require voters to select either "GOD—AND A RELIGIOUS PRESIDENT; or impiously declare for JEFFERSON—AND NO GOD!!!"

This widespread Federalist concern over Jefferson's lack of traditional religious belief gained credence from the efforts of prominent elements in the Jeffersonian coalition in states such as Massachusetts and Virginia to pull down the state-supported churches that those colonies had erected at the time of their earliest settlements. For people who lived in an age that had had little experience with societies that had maintained their stability without the assistance of such established churches, it was plausible to fear, as did a Federalist preacher in one 1800 election sermon, that if "the restraints of religion [were] once broken down, as they infallibly would be, by leaving the subject of public worship to the humors of the multitude, . . . we might well defy all human wisdom and power to support and preserve order and government in the State[s]."

If the Federalists were convinced that conferral of power upon Republicans would subvert morality and lead to violence and anarchy, the Republicans were equally convinced that, if allowed to retain power, the Federalists would subvert republican liberties and rule autocratically. These fears of a Federalist conspiracy to pervert American liberties came to a climax during the administration of President John Adams, who held office from 1797 to 1801. It was during his term that Congress for the first time in American history imposed a direct tax, voted to establish a standing army and navy, and adopted the Alien and Sedition Acts, pursuant to which Jeffersonian editors were sent to jail for criticizing government policies.

In short, clear-cut party divisions had emerged by the second half of the 1790s. On one side stood the Republicans, avowing in the words of James Madison "the doctrine that mankind are capable of governing themselves," and accused by their opponents of scheming "to introduce a new order of things as it respects *morals* and *politics*, *social* and *civil* duties." Opposite them stood the Federalists, claiming in the words of the *New England Palladium* to preserve "that virtue [which] is the only permanent basis of a Republic," and accused of attempting to restore monarchical government.

Both parties were internally divided, of course, and not everyone adhered rigidly to his party's ideology. Some statesmen continued to believe that popular will did not inevitably conflict with fundamental standards of right and that law and governmental policy could accordingly reflect both. Nonetheless, when forced to choose, those who styled themselves Federalists generally proclaimed their preference for customary standards, while those who saw themselves as Republicans generally proclaimed their allegiance to the people's will.

These two competing political theories were deeply rooted in still fresh American political experiences; they responded to ardently felt political needs. Republicans in 1800 could look back upon a quarter century of fervid political activity during which a majority of the people had transformed the American constitutional landscape. In light of this, Republicans could plausibly hold that the popular majority would secure revolutionary improvements in government through continued exertion.

Federalists, on the other hand, looked back on a different governmental tradition. They focused upon the workings of local government, which, even after twenty-five years of revolutionary transformation, continued to function without falling under the arbitrary control of those in positions of power. Federalists recognized a tradition, that is, of government by customary norms whose validity all right-thinking people accepted. That such traditional government seemed under attack in 1800 and unable to resolve every political issue was not startling; eighteenth-century government-by-consensus had always been somewhat unstable and unequipped to resolve all problems. Nevertheless, it had succeeded in many matters, and even its partial success offered hope to those in 1800 who dreaded government solely by majority will.

Marbury v. Madison came before the Supreme Court immediately after the conflict between these two approaches to politics had come to a head in the election of 1800, in which Thomas Jefferson defeated John Adams's reelection bid, and after John Marshall, *Marbury's* author, had been appointed in 1801 by the lame-duck Adams as chief justice of the United States. Before turning to *Marbury* itself, however, we need to examine the background of its author.

CHAPTER 3

John Marshall

John Marshall, who eventually would write the *Marbury v. Madison* opinion, was born in 1755 in the then frontier settlement of Germantown, in Prince William County, Virginia. He was the eldest of fifteen children of Mary Randolph Keith, who shared a common ancestry with leading Virginia families such as the Jeffersons, the Randolphs, and the Lees, and of Thomas Marshall, who was the American agent for Lord Fairfax, the British nobleman who owned immense tracts of land in northern Virgina. As a prominent member of his community, Thomas Marshall was active in its governance and served nearly continuously from 1759 until the American Revolution as a justice of the peace and at various times as county surveyor, sheriff, and parish vestryman. After 1769, he also represented his county, Fauquier, which had split off from Prince William, in the House of Burgesses.

As a youth, John Marshall thus was in a good position from which to observe the workings of Virginia's government. And upon attaining the age of twenty in 1775, he became a participant of sorts when he joined a militia unit in which his father held a position of command and marched off to Great Bridge, where he participated in a battle that drove the British army from Virginia soil. Seven months later, he accepted a commission as a lieutenant in the Continental army and spent the next four years at the side of his father's old friend, George Washington—at Valley Forge, among other places.

Marshall's military service was important to his subsequent career for three reasons. First, it turned him into a committed nationalist. As he worked with men from various parts of the new United States, he lost whatever parochialism he may have had and grew in appreciating the common interests of all Americans. Morevoer, as he watched his fellow soldiers suffer from lack of food and other supplies, especially at Valley Forge, he recognized the importance of a strong national government, having the capacity to furnish the military's needs.

Second, Marshall's service in the Continental army made him a protégé of George Washington. Washington promptly recognized Marshall's extraordinary talent, added him to his headquarters staff, and worked closely with him thereafter. Marshall, in turn, revered Washington as the great leader of the American cause, accepted political direction from Washington as long as the general lived, and ultimately became Washington's first biographer.

Third, the time that John Marshall spent in the army honed his skills as a leader and as a shaper of consensus. During his years of service, Marshall acted as a builder of morale and of dedication to the cause of American independence. He played that role, moreover, at a time when Continental officers had little coercive power over their troops and had to lead by example and by demonstrating fairness. Later, as chief justice of the United States, he would be in a comparable position. He would have little coercive power either over his fellow justices or over the nation as a whole, and he would have to build support for his judgments by convincing others that they were fair and sound and that they were derived from his allegiance to American liberty and constitutionalism.

Late in 1779, John Marshall was discharged from the army and went home to Virginia. Marshall quickly set his sights on becoming a lawyer and registered at the College of William and Mary for the law course taught by George Wythe, who had been Thomas Jefferson's law tutor and had been named to the first professorship of law in an American college during Jefferson's governorship of Virginia. Prior to attending Wythe's law lectures, Marshall had had little formal education: for one year, he had attended a school about one hundred miles from his home that was taught by a local clergyman, and then he had been tutored at home for an additional year by a recent college graduate from Britain. Nonetheless, by the end of the two years, Marshall was transcribing the poetry of Pope and reading Horace and Livy in Latin. Marshall also claimed that, prior to his entering military service at the age of twenty, he had been reading William Blackstone's four-volume *Commentaries on the Laws of England*.

Marshall studied at William and Mary during the spring and early summer of 1780. He compiled the usual set of notes for a law student, consisting of an alphabetical arrangement of information on various legal subjects that a practitioner would need when preparing for court appearances, and then set off in midsummer of 1780 to begin his practice in the new state capital of Richmond. There can be little doubt that John Marshall proved to be a lawyer of exceptional ability, and within the space of a few years, he had become one of the leading advocates—perhaps *the* leading advocate—in all of Virginia. Indeed, Marshall was so well respected that when Edmund Randolph was elected state governor in 1786, he urged his clients to turn to the young John Marshall, then only thirty-one years old, to be their attorney.

Meanwhile, Marshall had begun his political career. In 1782, Fauquier County, where he had grown up, elected him to the House of Delegates in the Virginia General Assembly. More significantly, when the assembly met, his fellow delegates, undoubtedly recognizing Marshall's unusual intellect and talent, elected him to the Governor's Privy Council, a body consisting largely of experienced state leaders, even though he was merely twenty-seven years old. In 1785, Marshall was elected an alderman of Richmond, his then place of residence, and his fellow aldermen then elected him recorder of the city, in which position he served for three years as a member of Richmond's municipal court, the Hustings Court.

Marshall's most important moments of public service in the 1780s came during the Virginia convention that had been called in 1788 to debate ratification of the proposed federal Constitution. Marshall was a key spokesman for the Federalist forces at the convention. The main task with which the Federalist leadership charged Marshall was the defense of the judiciary article of the Constitution and of the federal courts that, it was expected, Congress would create.

Marshall, in particular, tried to show that federal judges would be protectors of liberty rather than a threat to liberty. Most notably, he argued that the judiciary would guard against any attempt by Congress to enact legislation in excess of its delegated powers. As Marshall explained in anticipation of the *Marbury* decision some fifteen years later, if Congress "were to make a law not warranted by any of the powers enumerated, it would be considered by the judges as an infringement of the Constitution which they were to guard. . . . They would declare it void." Most historians have been of the view that Marshall's speeches in support of the Constitution were helpful in persuading the majority of delegates who secured ratification of the new government on the part of Virginia.

In view of his ability, his ties to Washington, and his services at the Virginia ratifying convention, Marshall undoubtedly was eligible for office under the new federal regime. But he did not want it. Instead, Marshall began the 1790s earning a handsome income from his burgeoning law practice, investing the proceeds in the Fairfax estate and other western land speculations, and assisting friends and family, especially his father, in their land speculations. His ambition was not the national and ultimately international fame that eventually would come his way, but rather the establishment of a great family, like those of the Jeffersons, the Randolphs, and the Lees, to which he was distantly related. In this ambition, he was typical of Virginians of his time.

Although he declined national office during the years of Washington's administration, Marshall nevertheless remained active in Virginia politics. From Virginia, he took strong stands in defense of President Washington and his administration, particularly of his foreign policy and of the treaty with England negotiated in 1794 by John Jay. His growing expertise on foreign affairs made him an obvious candidate for appointment to the three-man mission that President John Adams created in 1797 to negotiate a settlement to difficulties with the French Republic. Although he was unsure about accepting the assignment, Marshall ultimately decided to acquiesce out of an expectation that the mission would last only several months and that a brief absence would not interfere with his private law practice.

In the end, Marshall was absent from Virginia for slightly more than a year, and his efforts in Paris did not result in negotiation of a settlement. Nevertheless, the unsuccessful negotiation effort catapulted Marshall onto the national political stage as a hero.

Marshall's political success resulted from his superior understanding, which later would serve him well in his years as chief justice, of the workings of American democracy and constitutionalism. Upon meeting with French foreign minister Talleyrand, Marshall and his two fellow diplomats, who had come to negotiate issues regarding American neutrality and trade, were informed that the French government would not discuss those issues until the United States loaned $12 million to France and paid bribes to Talleyrand and other French officials totalling $250,000. Perhaps, Talleyrand did not appreciate what Marshall instinctively knew: that such sums could be paid only upon congressional appropriation* and that the American people never would permit Congress to appropriate funds for what appeared to be bribes and tribute. Armed with his knowledge, Marshall set out simply to lay before the American public a clear record of his transactions in France; he understood, as he wrote at the time, that the "mass" of his fellow citizens required "no more than to understand a question to decide it properly." Thus, he refused the French demands, made a public record of his refusal, and returned home as a hero.

Marshall's reports contributed to the building of anti-French sentiment in the United States, but Marshall himself continued to counsel moderation. In particular, he reported to President John Adams that he did not believe France wanted war with the United States and that war should be avoided. In his view, the French would negotiate once they realized that the American people supported their president.

* The sum of $12 million was a large one for 1798; all of the Louisiana Territory was purchased from France merely five years later for the slightly larger sum of $15 million.

The reasons for Marshall's moderation are unclear. Perhaps he had merely read the French accurately and was reporting to Adams intelligence that he had gathered in Paris. Alternatively, Marshall may have been reading his own home base of Richmond, Virginia, accurately: he knew that Virginians distrusted John Adams, he may have feared that they would not follow Adams into war, and he therefore may have urged Adams to preserve the Union by avoiding a war that could have fractured it. A third possibility is that Marshall was instinctively a man of moderation who strove to avoid unnecessary strife and create consensus among potential adversaries; as we shall see when we come to *Marbury v. Madison*, Marshall again pursued a course of moderation in dealing with that case.

Upon the conclusion of his French mission and his return to Richmond, Marshall wanted only to return to private law practice and to tend to his pecuniary affairs. Partisan politics, however, were growing hotter, and John Marshall's mentor, former President George Washington, thought it essential to get good Federalists elected to Congress. Accordingly, Washington summoned Marshall to Mount Vernon and informed him that it was his patriotic duty to run in the 1799 Virginia elections for Congress. Marshall ultimately performed his duty, as requested by Washington, and pursued a seat in Congress even after President Adams offered him a seat on the Supreme Court made vacant by the death of Justice James Wilson.

Marshall's campaign for Congress again illustrated his moderation, as well as his understanding of the workings of democratic politics. His key stand was his opposition to the Alien and Sedition Acts, which had been adopted by the Federalist Congress in order to make criminal and thereby stamp out newspaper criticism of the Adams administration but which had aroused strong resistance throughout the South, especially Virginia. Perhaps John Marshall thought it wrong to use the power of the national government against political opponents in the fashion authorized by the Alien and Sedition Acts, or perhaps he simply saw that he could not win election from his Richmond, Virginia, district unless he expressed opposition to the acts. For whatever reason, he was the only Federalist running for Congress who announced his opposition to the legislation, and he was one of the few Federalists who won election from the South.

Once he arrived at the nation's temporary capital of Philadelphia, Marshall's moderation and lawyerly skills made him one of the most important political leaders in town. The Federalist speaker of the House, Theodore Sedgwick, reported that Marshall possessed "great powers" and "much dexterity in the application of them" and that the Federalists could "do nothing without him." As a freshman, he was one of five congressmen named to committees considering a national bankruptcy act and an act enlarging the federal judiciary. He played an especially important role in connection with the first act, when he sought to soften opposition to the measure with an amendment calling for a jury trial on any issues of fact; without Marshall's amendment, the bankruptcy bill would not have passed the House, and the Bankruptcy Act of 1800 never would have become law.

Marshall also became the leading spokesman for President Adams in connection with the Thomas Nash affair. Nash, who had been one of a band of British sailors who had mutinied and murdered their officers, had been captured in Charleston, South Carolina, and extradited to Britain pursuant to the Jay Treaty, even though he had claimed to be an American citizen. Adams's opponents in Congress argued that Nash should not have been extradited until his claim of American citizenship had been adjudicated in court. Marshall, in a speech on the floor of the House, responded that the federal judiciary lacked jurisdiction in the Nash affair since there was no case or controversy between individual parties subject to judicial process and amenable to orders of the court; the dispute was between two sovereigns, Great Britain and the United States. When Congressman Albert Gallatin rose to rebut Marshall, he conceded instead that Marshall's argument was correct.*

* Marshall appears to have been wrong, in that the courts could have obtained jurisdiction if Nash had filed a writ of habeas corpus while in custody prior to his extradition. It is unclear why Nash did not seek habeas.

Marshall's political stock rose even further when, as Congress was about to adjourn in May 1800, divisions among the Federalists shattered the party. More extreme members of the party, responding to the leadership of Alexander Hamilton, deserted the Adams administration and provided little support for the president's 1800 reelection campaign. As a result of the desertion, two positions in the cabinet—secretary of war and secretary of state—became vacant.

John Marshall was a member of the more moderate wing of the party, which remained loyal to President Adams. As a result, Adams brought Marshall into the administration, when on May 7, 1800, he named Marshall as the new secretary of war. Marshall, however, never assumed the office because five days later, on May 12, 1800, Adams named him secretary of state.

Marshall's main duty as secretary of state was to preside over the conduct of American foreign policy. In performing this duty, he adhered to his own and the president's policy of maintaining peace with both Britain and France and thus steered a middle course between factional groups in America desiring war with one or the other.

Marshall also had some important domestic duties. The most important was his superintendence of the federal government's move from Philadelphia to its permanent capital of Washington, D.C. Another was drafting of President Adams's final annual message to Congress in December 1800, in which Marshall included a plea for reform of the judiciary. Through his ten months in the cabinet, John Marshall served as a trusted advisor to the president, who was in the midst of a reelection campaign against Thomas Jefferson and his Democratic-Republicans and who was also cut off from most of the leaders of his own Federalist Party, who regarded him as too moderate. Marshall was one of the few political figures who agreed with the policies of President Adams and was not eager to see the end of his term in office.

Nonetheless, despite his closeness to the president, John Marshall did not participate in the campaign of 1800. Instead, as we shall see, he preserved amicable relations with all sides, with the result that he had a pivotal role in postelectoral events during the winter of 1801.

As we saw in Chapter 2, John Adams lost the 1800 presidential race, but Thomas Jefferson did not emerge as the undisputed winner. Instead, Jefferson found himself tied for the lead in electoral votes with Aaron Burr, his running mate. Since no one candidate had an undisputed majority in the Electoral College, the choice between the two leaders, Jefferson and Burr, was thrown to the House of Representatives, where Federalists held the balance of power.

Marshall knew Thomas Jefferson, who was a distant cousin, well and distrusted him greatly. Thus, it is not surprising that late in December of 1800 Marshall wrote a letter to Charles Pinckney, the Federalist candidate for vice president, delicately suggesting to him that he use his influence with congressmen from his home state of South Carolina to persuade them to vote against Jefferson. Rumors abounded at the time of the letter that the Federalists would unite to prevent the election of any president or vice president, which would lead to a turnover of executive power either to the chief justice or to the ranking cabinet member, the secretary of state. Since the office of chief justice was vacant when Marshall wrote his letter, rumor suggested that Marshall himself would have assumed executive powers and become acting president if the House of Representatives had failed to consummate the election.

The letter to Pinckney was uncharacteristic of Marshall, however, and did not indicate the role he would play during the winter of 1801. Far more typical was his response to a letter he received from Alexander Hamilton, the leader of the extreme wing of the Federalist Party, which had deserted President Adams and undercut his reelection bid. Hamilton had been the rival of Thomas Jefferson ever since they had served together in the first cabinet of President Washington, but his rivalry in New York politics with Aaron Burr was even more vicious. In Hamilton's view, Jefferson was the lesser of two evils as president, and Hamilton accordingly began a campaign to induce the House of Representatives to select Jefferson rather than Burr as president. As part of that campaign,

Hamilton wrote a letter to Marshall, in which he stated his reasons for opposing Burr and urged Marshall to support Jefferson.

Marshall responded initially by noting his objections to Jefferson. Then he conceded that if Hamilton's description of Burr was accurate, the choice of Burr would be an even greater mistake than the selection of Jefferson. Marshall concluded his response by observing that, in light of Hamilton's representations, he no longer could favor Burr, but that at the same time he could "not bring myself to aid Mr. Jefferson." Accordingly, Marshall promised Hamilton that he would take no part in the business of selecting the next president.

The available evidence, in fact, indicates that after writing his letter to Hamilton, Marshall took no further part in the political battles that ultimately led to Thomas Jefferson's election as president. Instead, he adopted an approach, which he would later bring to the American judiciary, of standing aside from partisan conflict, of doing his own work, and of letting the democratic political process take its own course. He remained neutral.

Marshall also left no evidence that he played any role in his own selection as chief justice, which occurred less than a month before the House of Representatives finally broke the Jefferson-Burr tie. The office of chief justice of the United States had become vacant when Oliver Ellsworth, the incumbent, became ill and in December 1800 submitted his resignation to President Adams. Adams initially offered the position to John Jay, who had been the first chief justice and was a loyal Federalist and a lawyer and statesman of distinction. However, Jay, who had once resigned from the job, declined reappointment, and in January 1801, he so informed the president.

At that point, two sitting justices appeared to be the most obvious candidates for the office. The one was William Cushing, the senior associate justice and an old colleague of Adams from Massachusetts in times before and during the War of Independence, when they had both been lawyers and judges. The other was William Paterson of New Jersey, who had been a leading figure at the 1787 Constitutional Convention and later a senator from his state. The objection to Cushing was his age, which was sixty-

nine; the objection to Paterson was Adams's unwillingness to pre-
fer him over his old friend Cushing as well as Paterson's support
for the Hamilton wing of the Federalist Party rather than for
Adams in the election of 1800.

Marshall himself supported the appointment of Paterson, and
when he presented Adams with Jay's letter declining appointment,
he proposed Paterson's name. But Adams responded in no uncertain terms that he would not appoint Paterson. It was also clear
that Cushing's age barred his appointment. The result was that
Adams was in a bind. Less than six weeks remained in his administration, and, if he failed to appoint a new chief justice, Thomas
Jefferson or Aaron Burr would make the appointment, and the
Federalists' opportunity to dominate the Supreme Court during
the years to come would lapse. Adams did not have time to canvass
the nation by the slow mails of 1801 to determine whether leading
Federalists wished to assume the office. He had to offer the chief
justiceship to someone close at hand who would either accept it or
reject it quickly enough so that he could then offer it to someone
else.

As the secretary of state in the Adams administration, John
Marshall was close at hand. Adams also knew of Marshall's intelligence and general level of ability, as well as his loyalty to Adams's
vision of federalism and his political moderation. Accordingly,
Adams nominated Marshall.

Marshall immediately accepted, but the Federalists in Congress
were astounded. Marshall was young (only forty-five years of age
at the time) and had rebelled against party discipline, and his appointment meant that older, more distinguished, and more reliable
Federalists were being passed over. For this reason, the Senate de-
layed confirmation of Marshall for a week. But, although some
Federalists remained hesitant even though only five weeks remained in the Adams administration, the choice of John Marshall as chief justice of the United States was finally confirmed by
the Senate, in part because of the enthusiastic support of all fifteen Jeffersonian Republicans, who admired Marshall's rebellions
against party discipline as well as his general moderation. On
February 4, 1801—precisely one month before Thomas Jefferson

was sworn in as president—Marshall took his seat as chief justice. Little business was conducted during the 1801 term, however, and no decisions were handed down.

Meanwhile, at Adams's request, Marshall remained on for the final month of the administration as the acting secretary of state. As such, he became actively involved in the transfer of power from Adams to Jefferson once it became clear in mid-February 1801 that Jefferson would be the next president. Thus, he advised American diplomats overseas to delay engaging in negotiations or making other decisions that might bind the new Jefferson administration to policies it might not accept.

Marshall also sought to move beyond the harsh rhetoric of the electoral campaign and to restore greater civility to relationships between the two political parties. Thus, when Jefferson informed Marshall that he had no one to help him prepare the various messages he would need to give at the outset of his administration, Marshall promptly assigned the chief clerk of the State Department to work with the president-elect.

Both Jefferson and Marshall recognized the importance of a peaceful, orderly transition of power after the hotly fought 1800 election. Such a transition had never occurred before in American history, and Jefferson and Marshall worked together to bring it about. Whatever Marshall's fears of Jefferson may have been as late as December 1800, Marshall was willing to give Jefferson the benefit of the doubt in the days before his inauguration and to anticipate that the "public prosperity and happiness" would "sustain no diminution under democratic guidance." Although Marshall continued to distrust some of Jefferson's partisan supporters, he indicated in a letter written on inauguration day that he did not distrust the president-elect himself.

Thus, when Jefferson requested Marshall to administer the presidential oath of office at noon on March 4, 1801, Marshall promptly agreed. He appears to have appreciated fully the symbolic significance of having the highest-ranking officeholder of the outgoing Federalist Party, which he became when John Adams left Washington, D.C., on the morning of the inauguration, swear in the new president as the leader of the opposing Democratic-

Republican Party. Jefferson, in turn, reciprocated by delivering a conciliatory inaugural address and by asking Marshall to remain on as secretary of state for a few extra days until James Madison, his successor, arrived in town.

Thus, it is essential to understand that as John Marshall assumed the bench following one of the most ferocious political fights in American history, he was no fanatic. On the contrary, he was a moderate who understood the importance of allowing the democratic political process to follow its course. His goal was to bring people together and to restore harmony and consensus, not to divide them further and thereby lead them to violence and bloodshed. It is against the background of this moderation that we must understand *Marbury v. Madison*, the landmark opinion that Marshall delivered only two years after his ascension to the bench and Jefferson's assumption of the presidency.

CHAPTER 4

Marbury and the Crisis of 1801–1803

Although Jefferson and Marshall behaved in a conciliatory fashion toward each other in an effort to effectuate a peaceful transition of power on March 4, 1801, other Federalists and Republicans remained more partisan. Among the more partisan were the Federalist leaders of the lame-duck Congress that met in December 1800 and promptly enacted the Judiciary Act of 1801, which revamped the lower federal judiciary. The act expanded the jurisdiction of the federal courts and created a number of new federal judgeships, which President Adams, in his closing days in office, filled entirely with Federalists, who came to be known as midnight judges, from the belated nature of their appointments.

To appreciate the significance of the 1801 act, it is necessary to focus on the role of federal courts in the constitutional order. Unlike government today, late-eighteenth- and early-nineteenth-century government did not possess a large bureaucracy capable of enforcing the law and bringing its will to bear on local communities. Judges constituted the only body of officials through which central governing authorities could have a presence in localities.

Under the Articles of Confederation, no federal courts had existed, except for a Court of Appeals in Admiralty Cases, which had reviewed several state trial court judgments, all of them involving the capture of British vessels by American privateers during the course of the War for Independence. All other cases involving national law or national policy began and ended in the state courts, with no possibility of appeal to any national court.

Thus, the Confederation Congress, in effect, was totally dependent on state judges to enforce national law, and it was easy to anticipate, if national law and state policy were inconsistent, that state judges would not enforce national law, such as the rule proclaimed by the peace treaty that had ended the Revolutionary War that British creditors would suffer no impediments to the collection of their debts. Americans seeking a strong national government, either on general principles or in order to enforce specific national policies—and nearly all members of the Federalist Party in 1800 fit within either the one or the other category—therefore sought the creation of federal courts, preferably with original as well as appellate jurisdiction, to perform the task, as no other institution could, of enforcing national policies.

The Philadelphia Convention reached a compromise when it drafted the Constitution itself in 1787. The convention mandated the creation of a Supreme Court, to which litigants in either state courts or lower federal courts could take an appeal in any case involving federal law. The Supreme Court, however, possesses only limited power to enforce national law, since many litigants will be unable to appeal cases to it and even when appeals are taken, lower courts will not always enforce the Supreme Court's mandates. Lower federal courts thus are essential to comprehensive enforcement of national law, but in respect to lower courts, the Philadelphia Convention compromised, as it left to future Congresses decisions about whether to create any lower federal courts and, if it created them, about the scope of their jurisdiction.

Even with this compromise, however, Americans who began to style themselves Antifederalists were troubled by the provisions of the Constitution dealing with the judiciary and levied attacks on those provisions during the ratification debates. Antifederalists worried that federal courts posed a threat to local liberties. Familiar with a world in which state-court juries had power to determine law as well as fact and thus block the enforcement of national policies in any locality that did not accept them, the Antifederalists feared that Congress might create federal courts in which judges determined law and fact; such federal courts would weaken the power of the states to nullify federal policy.

The Bill of Rights responded, in part, to these Antifederalist concerns—especially to concerns that juries might be weakened or even eliminated from a new federal judicial system. First, the

Seventh Amendment guaranteed the right to trial by jury in all civil cases in which the amount in controversy exceeded twenty dollars. Second, the right to jury trial in criminal cases, which had been preserved in the original Constitution, was further protected in the Sixth Amendment by the guarantee that the jury would be drawn from the district wherein the alleged crime had been committed. Third, the Bill of Rights guaranteed that no fact found by a jury could be reexamined by a judge, except to the extent allowed at common law.

But the Bill of Rights constituted a compromise rather than a capitulation to Antifederalist demands. The Sixth and Seventh Amendments protected the control of juries over fact-finding, but they did not place the power of juries to find law beyond change by Congress or the judiciary. Thus, the amendments left open the possibility that a powerful federal judiciary could overturn jury nullification of federal law and thereby enforce federal policies in recalcitrant states.

The First Congress continued the policy of compromise in its decisions regarding the creation of a national judiciary. The Judiciary Act of 1789 established only a meager federal judiciary and gave it only limited jurisdiction, in particular over cases between litigants from different states. The 1789 act did not give jurisdiction, however, over all matters of federal law to the federal courts. Moreover, it created only two sorts of judges, Supreme Court and district judges, and it provided that federal circuit courts, which were granted most of the jurisdiction conferred by the act, would consist of one district judge and two Supreme Court judges riding circuit. Since each Supreme Court judge might be required to sit on circuit courts in at least five different locations, the 1789 act guaranteed that the principal federal trial courts could meet only infrequently and could not rival state judges and state juries as institutions for resolution of the great mass of legal disputes. Finally, the act allowed most civil litigants to bring cases to federal courts only when they were seeking a judgment of at least $500—a large amount for 1789 and an amount that ensured that most Americans would never be summoned into a federal court as a defendant.

Thus, when the lame-duck Federalist Congress assembled in

December 1800, it met against the background of over a decade of conflict about the existence, size, and jurisdiction of the federal judiciary—conflict that had been resolved through compromises that had created a meager and somewhat inconsequential system of federal courts. The Judiciary Act of 1801 upset these compromises. It gave federal courts jurisdiction to hear all cases involving questions of federal law and, in addition, lowered from $500 to $100 the minimum amount of money that a plaintiff had to claim in order to bring a federal suit.

As a result of these changes, many more Americans could have been summoned into federal courts. Moreover, the 1801 act made those courts more efficient. In particular, it created sixteen new circuit judges, who collectively would have had a substantially greater capacity to determine lawsuits than the six Supreme Court judges who had been riding circuit under the 1789 act.

The midnight judges appointed by President Adams only exacerbated the concerns of those opposed to expanding the federal courts. The Judiciary Act of 1801 became law on February 13—less than three weeks before John Adams's term as president expired. Undaunted, however, Adams managed to appoint and obtain Senate confirmation for sixteen new circuit judges, all of them Federalists, as well as for several judges of courts, newly created by an act of February 27, 1801, in the District of Columbia. Unfortunately, Secretary of State Marshall was unable to deliver the commission for one of the new justices of the peace for the district, a certain William Marbury, before the end of President Adams's term, and James Madison, the new secretary of state, refused to make the uncompleted delivery. Upon his refusal, Marbury brought a suit for a writ of mandamus* against Madison in the Supreme Court, and thus the case of *Marbury v. Madison* began.

---

* A writ of mandamus (which obtains its name from the Latin verb *mandamus*, which means "we order") is a document issued by a court that orders a defendant, in this case Secretary of State Madison, to perform a specified act, in this case to deliver a commission, on behalf of a specified plaintiff, in this case William Marbury.

But before the Court could hear the case, Congress, now under the control of the Jeffersonian Republicans, intervened and passed the Judiciary Act of 1802, which repealed the Judiciary Act of 1801. Cases pending in the new circuit courts established under the 1801 act were transferred by the 1802 legislation back to the old circuit courts that had existed under the 1789 act. Congress also postponed the next term of the Supreme Court until 1803 so that the Court could not rule on the constitutionality of the 1802 act before the act went into effect.

Nonetheless, in one case so transferred, *Stuart v. Laird*, the defendant argued that the 1802 repeal act, and hence the transfer of his case, was unconstitutional. When his argument was rejected in the lower court, he appealed to the Supreme Court. Decided only six days after *Marbury*, *Stuart* became, in effect, a companion case in determining the legitimacy of the judicial policies of both Federalists and Republicans during the transition from the Adams to the Jefferson administration.

Marbury v. Madison and *Stuart v. Laird*, both decided in 1803, thus created the possibility of a direct confrontation between the Federalist judiciary left over from the Adams administration and the new Jeffersonian Congress. In such a confrontation, Congress would have been very much on the offensive. As one Republican newspaper, the *Boston Independent Chronicle*, warned in 1803, any attempt "of federalism to exalt the Judiciary over the Executive and Legislature, and to give that favorite department a political character & influence" would "terminate in the degradation and disgrace of the judiciary." However, Chief Justice Marshall, by nature a compromiser, was not inclined to take up this Republican challenge and generate a clash with President Jefferson and his Republican Congress.

John Marshall had no propensity to turn *Marbury* and *Stuart* into instances of judicial review of the sort that the Jeffersonians feared. Although Chief Justice Marshall was prepared, as he wrote, to "disregard" the pressures of partisan politics when they were "put in competition with . . . his duty" to uphold the law, and although he always kept in mind the desirability of adjudicating at least some matters by a nonmajoritarian standard and thereby restraining "the capricious *will* of the rulers of the day," he and his fellow Federalist justices, with the possible exception of Justice Samuel Chase, were not elitist antidemocrats. They appreciated the need to steer clear of partisan controversy and not to challenge unnecessarily legislation enacted by democratic majorities. As Marshall's private correspondence with his colleagues in the opening years of the 1800s indicates, the chief justice and his colleagues were fully aware of "[t]he consequences of refusing to carry . . . into effect" a law enacted by a popular majority.

Marshall and the other justices, in short, strove to reconcile popular will and legal principle, not to make one either superior or subservient to the other. They had no intention to behave as the Supreme Court ultimately would in *Cooper v. Aaron*, a 1958 school desegregation case in which the Court for the first time in its history explicitly arrogated to itself the exclusive power to interpret the Constitution. Unlike the justices in *Cooper*, Marshall and his colleagues did not declare themselves to be the ultimate arbiters of the nation's constitutional policy choices, with power to bind coordinate branches of government to their judgments of constitutionality and thereby invalidate popularly supported legislative politics inconsistent with the constitutional values they favored. *Marbury v. Madison* and *Stuart v. Laird* would be much narrower decisions.

John Marshall and the other Federalist justices achieved their narrow goals in *Marbury* and *Stuart* by distinguishing between the domain of law and the domain of politics. Indeed, the foundation of Marshall's constitutional jurisprudence is the distinction between political matters, to be resolved by the legislative and executive branches in the new democratic, majoritarian style, and legal matters, to be resolved by the judiciary in the government-by-consensus style that had prevailed in most eighteenth-century American courts. Marshall, of course, invented neither style, nor did he first apply the latter to the adjudicatory process. His creative act was to use the distinction between law and politics to circumscribe, however imperfectly, the extent to which the political, majoritarian style could engulf all government, as it was threatening in 1800 to do.

Merely announcing a line between law and politics does not, of course, fully differentiate the legal from the political. It is also necessary to put content into the line by articulating consistent and precise criteria for identifying matters appropriately decided by the legal method. We need to examine both *Marbury v. Madison* and *Stuart v. Laird* in considerable detail to appreciate how John Marshall and his fellow justices accomplished this difficult task.

Marshall began the *Marbury* opinion with a narrow and technical ruling—that President Adams's signature on Marbury's commission completed Marbury's appointment to the office of justice of the peace and entitled him to the delivery of his commission. This ruling was especially important, however, because for lawyers of Marshall's generation a right to an office was analogous to a right to land or other property. It meant that Marbury possessed "a vested legal right" to his commission, and it led the chief justice to the second issue in his opinion—did Marbury have a remedy for the deprivation of the right?

When summoned before the Court in the preliminary stages of the case, Department of State officers had claimed not only that Marbury had no remedy for the delivery of his commission, but also that they were privileged, by virtue of their executive status, not to testify about any transactions concerning the commission. Marshall recognized this as a potentially far-reaching claim, for if the government asserted such a privilege in matters involving land patents, which Marshall and lawyers of his time, as we have seen, thought analogous to commissions for office, it would cloud the title to much of the land west of the Appalachians. Unfounded fears had intensified the political divisions of 1800, and, whatever the truth may have been, the Federalist Court doubtless feared that Thomas Jefferson's new administration might claim to be above the law in these matters as well as others. Marshall's real difficulty was that he, unlike more extreme Federalists, could not summarily reject the claim of executive privilege, for as he had once told his constituents, he believed that the people, and hence their agents in the political branches of government, must sometimes be free to act unbound by fixed legal principles.

Accordingly his central task in *Marbury* was to specify when law bound the political branches and when it did not. To do so, he and the Court distinguished between political matters, such as foreign policy, as to which the legislature and executive were accountable only to the electorate, and matters of individual rights, which the courts would protect by adhering to fixed principles. In Marshall's own words, "political" subjects "respect[ed] the nation, not individual rights" and were governed by a political branch whose decisions were "never . . . examinable by the courts" but "only politically examinable."

In contrast, there were cases where "a specific duty [was] assigned by law, and individual rights depend[ed] upon the performance of that duty." In such cases involving "the rights of individuals," every officer of government was "amenable to the laws for his conduct; and [could not] at his discretion sport away . . . vested rights," and a person, such as Marbury, who possessed a vested right was entitled to a remedy. In Marshall's own words, "[t]he very essence of civil liberty certainly consist[ed] in the right of every individual to claim the protection of the laws, whenever he receives an injury."

Thus, William Marbury was entitled to some remedy for deprivation of his right to office. But was he entitled to the particular remedy he had sought—a writ of mandamus issued by the Supreme Court of the United States in a suit commenced before it? The Judiciary Act of 1789 authorized the Court to issue writs of mandamus, but the judiciary article of the Constitution presented a problem, in that it limited the original jurisdiction of the Supreme Court to specified categories of cases, of which mandamus was not one. In order for the Court to issue the writ, it thus would have to reach one of two conclusions: either that Congress had power to grant original jurisdiction to the Supreme Court in cases in which the Constitution denied it, or that an action for mandamus in the Supreme Court was not the commencement of an original proceeding but a form of appeal from the official against whom the writ was being sought.

It is noteworthy that Marbury's counsel did not press the argument that by granting mandamus in a suit commenced before it the Supreme Court exercised its original jurisdiction over original matters not specified in the Constitution. Instead, he mainly argued that the Court exercised appellate jurisdiction when issuing mandamus in a proceeding commenced before it. According to the thrust of his argument, which flowed from an accurate reading of *Federalist* Number 81, "the word 'appellate' [was] not to be taken in its technical sense, . . . but in its broadest sense, in which it denotes nothing more than the power of one tribunal" to have "by reason of its supremacy . . . the superintendence of . . . inferior tribunals and officers, whether judicial or ministerial." In 1803, when the concept of appeal had not yet assumed its relatively narrow and precise modern meaning, that argument was plausible, and a court anxious to grant Marbury relief could easily have accepted it.

However, accepting the argument would have contradicted Marshall's distinction between matters of political discretion and matters of legal right, for it would have frequently led the Court to "revis[e] and correct the proceedings in a cause already instituted" in the executive branch and might thereby have brought before the Court all the issues, both of law and of fact, that the executive branch had previously considered. Such review might have continually presented the Court with political questions of executive motive. To avoid this danger and to ensure that the court serve as the purely legal institution he envisioned, Marshall had to consider a mandamus against officials, as distinguished from a mandamus against lower-court judges, as an original action in which the court granting the writ could confine the action's scope to properly legal rather than political matters. Thus, he had to reject the claim that mandamus was a direct appeal from the executive to the Supreme Court.

That brought Chief Justice Marshall to the issue whether Congress could grant the Supreme Court jurisdiction that the Constitution denied it. Note how, so far in his opinion, Marshall and his fellow justices had underscored the distinction between law and politics. They had held, as did then existing case law, that once the President appointed Marbury to a judicial office, Marbury had a property right in that office and was entitled to a legal remedy through which to enforce the right. They also had ruled that an appeal from the secretary of state's refusal to deliver Marbury's commission was the wrong remedy, since such an appeal would have brought the discretionary concerns that had prompted the secretary's refusal before the Court and thus would have embroiled the Court in a political rather than purely legal matter.

But how could Marshall and his fellow justices complete their *Marbury* opinion without exercising political judgment and thereby becoming entangled in politics? To grant an original writ of mandamus directing Secretary of State Madison to put Marbury in office would have forced a confrontation between the Court and the Jefferson administration, which could have ended at best with Madison's refusal to obey the Court's order and at worst with Congress's impeachment of Chief Justice John Marshall and his subsequent conviction and removal from office. Thus, Marshall had to find a way to deny Marbury the writ of mandamus he was seeking. The way he found was to declare unconstitutional Congress's grant of jurisdiction to the Court, in the Judiciary Act of 1789, to issue original writs of mandamus. This recourse to judicial review, however, strikes readers at the outset of the twenty-first century as perhaps even more political than granting the writ to Marbury would have been.

But Marshall did not understand judicial review as we do today. For Marshall and his colleagues on the Supreme Court, judicial review neither required nor permitted judges to exercise political discretion. In that familiar portion of the *Marbury* opinion which asserts the power of judicial review, Marshall reiterated his belief in "the fundamental principles" of law that were "designed to be permanent." But at no point in the opinion did he invoke the language of natural rights, nor did he rely on precedent or other prior judicial authority. In fact, he cited only one case in his entire opinion. In short, Marshall never relied upon principles that either were made by or required interpretation by judges. On the contrary, the principles that he found fundamental acquired their authority from the "original right" of the people "to establish, for their future government, such principles as, in their opinion, shall most conduce to their own happiness." In so ruling, the Marshall

Court evoked the Revolutionary generation's assumption that the people, acting as a unitary body rather than as disparate individuals, had incorporated basic and generally agreed-upon principles of right into their Constitution. The Court thereby reverted to something like the governance by consensus techniques of its eighteenth-century predecessors.

For Marshall and his colleagues, judicial review merely required comparison of fundamental principles incorporated by the people into the written text of the Constitution (which in the case of *Marbury* conferred original jurisdiction on the Supreme Court only in specified categories of cases and declared its jurisdiction to be appellate in all other cases) with the text of legislation (which gave the Court original jurisdiction over a category not within the Constitution's specifications). As the *Marbury* opinion declared, it was

> emphatically the province and duty of the judicial department to say what the law is. . . . If two laws conflict[ed] with each other, the courts must decide on the operation of each.
>
> So if a law be in opposition to the constitution; if both the law and the constitution apply to a particular case, so that the court must either decide that case conformably to the law, disregarding the constitution; or conformably to the constitution, disregarding the law; the court must determine which of these conflicting rules governs the case. This is of the very essence of judicial duty.
>
> If then, . . . the constitution is superior to any ordinary act of the legislature, the constitution, and not such ordinary act, must govern the case to which they both apply.
>
> Those then who controvert the principle that the constitution is to be considered, in court, as a paramount law, are reduced to the necessity of maintaining that courts must close their eyes on the constitution, and see only the law.
>
> This doctrine would subvert the very foundation of all written constitutions. It would declare that an act which, according to the principles and theory of our government, is entirely

void, is yet, in practice, completely obligatory. It would declare that if the legislature shall do what is expressly forbidden, such act, notwithstanding the express prohibition, is in reality effectual. It would be giving to the legislature a practical and real omnipotence, with the same breath which professes to restrict their powers within narrow limits. It is prescribing limits, and declaring that those limits may be passed at pleasure.

That it thus reduces to nothing what we have deemed the greatest improvement on political institutions—a written constitution— . . . [is] sufficient, in America, where written constitutions have been viewed with so much reverence for rejecting the construction.

The Supreme Court's approach in *Marbury v. Madison* was not new, of course; *Federalist* Number 78 had formulated it much earlier. There Alexander Hamilton had written:

Some perplexity respecting the right of the courts to pronounce legislative acts void, because contrary to the constitution, has arisen from an imagination that the doctrine would imply a superiority of the judiciary to the legislative power. It is urged that the authority which can declare the acts of another void, must necessary be superior to the one whose acts may be declared void.

But, Hamilton declared, it would be wrong so to imply judicial superiority. On the contrary, it was

far more rational to suppose that the courts were designed to be an intermediate body between the people and the legislature, in order, among other things, to keep the latter within the limits assigned to their authority. The interpretation of the laws is the proper and peculiar function of the courts. A constitution is in fact, and must be, regarded by the judges as a fundamental law. It therefore belongs to them to ascertain its meaning as well as the meaning of any particular act proceeding from the legislative body. If there should happen to be an irreconcileable variance between the two, that which has the superior obligation and validity ought of course to be preferred; or in other words, the constitution ought to be preferred to the statute, the intention of the people to the intention of their agents.

Nor does this conclusion by any means suppose of superiority of the judicial to the legislative power. It only supposes that the power of the people is superior to both; and that where the will of the legislature declared in its statutes, stands in opposition to that of the people declared in the constitution, the judges ought to be governed by the latter, rather than the former. They ought to regulate their decisions by the fundamental laws, rather than by those which are not fundamental.

Hamilton, in turn, was merely following ideas that had been expressed earlier by delegates at the Constitutional Convention or elsewhere during the ratification debates. Thus, Luther Martin, a delegate from Maryland, had noted at the Philadelphia Convention that, "as to the Constitutionality of laws, that point will come before the Judges . . . [, and] they will have a negative on the laws," while Patrick Henry, the leader of the antiratification forces in Virginia, had declared during that state's ratification debates that it was "the highest encomium of this country, that the acts of the legislature, if unconstitutional, are liable to be opposed by the judiciary." Clearest of all had been Elbridge Gerry, a delegate from Massachusetts, who had taken note at Philadelphia of the judiciary's "power of deciding on the . . . Constitutionality" of laws. "In some states," as Gerry accurately reported, "the judges had actually set aside laws as being against the Constitution. This was done too with general approbation."

Indeed, John Marshall himself had written during the 1780s of certain "maxims of democracy," which ought to be enforced by judges and which included "[a] strict observance of justice and public faith, and a steady adherence to virtue." And during the Virginia ratification convention, as we have seen, Marhsall had warned that if Congress "were to make a law not warranted by any of the powers enumerated, it would be considered by the Judges as an infringement of the Constitution which they are to guard:

—They would not consider such a law as coming under their jurisdiction. —They would declare it void."

Of course, the propriety of exercising the power of judicial review was not without doubt prior to *Marbury v. Madison*. Opposition to judicial review had arisen in some states, most notably Rhode Island, after judges had utilized the power, and Hamilton had found it necessary to write *Federalist* Number 78 precisely because a leading Antifederalist, Robert Yates, had plausibly warned that judges who made political judgments in the exercise of judicial review would in fact become policy makers with practical superiority over the legislature.

Still, whatever ambiguity may have existed, the Marshall Court's assumption of the power of judicial review was hardly unprecedented. No one, of course, wanted the Court to assume policy-making powers. But the Chief Justice gave adequate reassurance that it would not when he announced that the Court would consider only legal and not political issues and then struggled, in those portions of the *Marbury* opinion that we now tend to ignore, to articulate a standard that would minimize the Court's political involvement.

Thus, the distinction between legal and political decision making runs throughout the *Marbury* opinion and is essential to our understanding of the case. It explains, for example, how Marshall could plausibly believe that judicial review involved not an exercise of political discretion by the Court, but merely a juxtaposing of statute with Constitution to see if they conflicted. When the Court could resolve a case according to seemingly fixed principles rather than transient policies, Marshall believed judicial review fell on the law side of the distinction and involved merely the judiciary's judicial protection of immutable, individual rights. In contrast, a case that required the Court to choose among transient policies or otherwise to exercise political discretion was not in Marshall's estimation an appropriate case for judicial review.

The distinction between law and politics outlined in *Marbury* gained force six days later from the Court's disposition of the other pending case that questioned the constitutionality of an act of Congress. *Stuart v. Laird* passed upon the Republicans' Judiciary Act of 1802, which repealed the Federalists' Judiciary Act of 1801.

Federalists had contended in Congress that the 1802 act was unconstitutional because it deprived judges appointed under the 1801 act of the lifetime tenure guaranteed by article III, section 1, of the Constitution. The 1802 act was also said to be unconstitutional because it required Supreme Court justices to sit as trial judges in circuit courts, thereby conferring an original jurisdiction that, the argument contended, only the Constitution could confer. *Marbury*, we ought to recall, had been decided on an almost identical ground.

Nonetheless, the Marshall Court sustained the 1802 act. The apparent inconsistency between *Marbury* and *Stuart*, however, masks a deeper consistency in the Court's approach. Significantly, the court in *Stuart* never faced the contention that would have most troubled it: that the 1802 act unconstitutionally deprived judges of a right to hold office. That contention would have involved issues of legally enforceable private rights, but it was not even raised, for Stuart was not one of the judges deprived of office; he was merely a litigant objecting to the transfer of his case from a court constituted under the 1801 act to a court constituted under the 1802 act. His complaint raised no issue of fundamental private rights, only issues of Congress's political power to organize the lower federal courts.

There were two such issues. First, could Congress require a litigant to pursue his remedies in one court rather than another? As Marshall would suggest twenty-four years later in *Ogden v. Saunders*, the legislature clearly could control remedies. Second, could Congress require Supreme Court justices to ride circuit and thereby exercise an original jurisdiction not enumerated in the Constitution?

Marbury had decided, of course, that Congress could not expand the Supreme Court's original jurisdiction, but *Stuart* could be distinguished from *Marbury*, in that the 1802 Judiciary Act required individual justices, not the full Court, to exercise original jurisdiction. Further, as Justice Paterson explained for the unanimous Court, the 1802 act merely confirmed "practice and acquiescence" by Supreme Court justices "commencing with the organization of the judicial system." Such practice and acquiescence "afford[ed] an irresistible answer" to the claim of unconstitutionality; it was a "practical exposition . . . too strong and obstinate to be shaken or controlled," and "indeed fixed the construction" of the Constitution. The fact that the justices had performed the circuit duties imposed under the 1789 Judiciary Act put "the question . . . at rest." In *Marbury*, on the other hand, no strong public sentiment, precedent, or established practice stood in the way of holding that the Constitution's language prohibited the issuance of mandamus as a matter of original jurisdiction.

But a more fundamental fact distinguished *Marbury* from *Stuart*. By invalidating the Republican-sponsored Judiciary Act of 1802, the Marshall Court would have embroiled itself in a political contest with Congress and the president that it might not have survived. If the Court was to withdraw from politics, as Marshall had said in *Marbury* it would, it had to capitulate to legislative judgments upon such politically controversial issues as the constitutionality of the 1802 act. Accordingly, the Court sustained the act.

By contrast, the only way to avoid the politics behind *Marbury* had been to construe the Constitution in a way to which few would object, and thereby invalidate section 13 of the 1789 Judiciary Act. To have issued a writ of mandamus to James Madison as secretary of state would have thrust the court into a political crisis. The Court's only other option—to hold on substantive grounds that Marbury had no right to the mandamus—would have denied some individuals access to the courts to enforce their legal rights. In short, to maintain Marshall's compromise—that courts would protect legal rights but refrain from adjudicating political questions—the Court had to decide both *Marbury* and *Stuart* as it did.

Thus, in two of the earliest cases decided by the Supreme Court following the 1800 election, Chief Justice John Marshall and the other Federalist justices on the Court publicly addressed the task of reconciling popular will, which had provided the basis for the Jeffersonian-Republican victory in the election, and immutable principles, in which they, as well as many fellow citizens, continued to place their faith. As such, *Marbury* and *Stuart* were central to the process of differentiating law from politics and declaring that the Supreme Court would abstain from the exercise of political judgment.

Although many historians will disagree, I remain convinced that judicial review was able to take root in early-nineteenth-century America only because Marshall and his contemporaries believed, at some level, that the principles underlying constitutional government were nonpolitical—that is, that those principles existed independently of the will of the judges who applied them as well as the will of the political actors who flouted them. Of course, their belief was largely unarticulated, since they found its articulation as difficult as we find it to spell out our comparable beliefs. But at the same time that the principles underlying *Marbury* were largely unarticulated, they also were unproblematic because political elites, the only people who discussed such issues, accepted the justices' views. When elements of the elite did not agree with the Marshall Court's views—as, for instance, on issues of the scope of federal and state powers—the Court refused to act in an independent political fashion and to impose its own views but merely enforced the legislation that had been adopted by the majority of the Congress.

It is essential to emphasize, however, that by eschewing independent political decision making the Court did not entirely remove itself from the political process. Cases as politically controversial as *Marbury* and *Stuart* still continued to find their way onto the Supreme Court's docket, and the Court continued to decide them. The justices also continued to behave strategically, as Marshall had in *Marbury*, where in dictum he proclaimed the Court's authority to enforce the law, lectured the president for violating it, and then turned to the less controversial doctrine of judicial review as the foundation for a judgment acceptable both to the president and to Congress. But until it invalidated the Missouri Compromise in *Scott v. Sandford* some fifty-four years after

Marbury, the Court never struck down a legislative policy judgment for which a substantial nationwide political majority had voted and to which many voters in the polity still adhered. In that sense, the Marshall Court in *Marbury v. Madison* took itself out of politics.

CHAPTER 5

The Early Impact of *Marbury*

For several decades after *Marbury v. Madison*, the assumptions of Chief Justice Marshall and his fellow justices about the nonpolitical character of judicial review provided an adequate foundation for the practice in state courts as well as the Supreme Court. As we shall see in this chapter, judicial review was uncontroversial in the early nineteenth century.

As soon as the Supreme Court had handed down its decisions in *Marbury v. Madison* and *Stuart v. Laird*, most political observers recognized the importance of the two cases. Both Federalist and Republican newspapers took note of the decisions and apprised readers of their significance. Some newspapers even published the *Marbury* opinion verbatim. The politically active segments of the American public fully understood John Marshall's efforts at compromise.

On the whole, Americans also appreciated Marshall's efforts. Although President Jefferson in later years would privately criticize the *Marbury* decision, he did not criticize it at the time the decision came down. Likewise, there was no criticism from Congress, which happened to be in session at the time of the decision. Similarly the Republican press, while giving extensive coverage to the decision, refrained from attacking it, while the Federalist press was, of course, supportive. Although the Marshall Court would later decide contentious issues and become engulfed in controversy, there was a general consensus that the Court had correctly decided both *Marbury v. Madison* and *Stuart v. Laird*. Only the political fringes of the Jeffersonian and Federalist parties had any doubts about the two decisions.

Why, we need to ask, did *Marbury* and *Stuart* seem so important and at the same time generate so little controversy? Several explanations come to the surface. First, the *Marbury* and *Stuart* decisions were modest ones that withdrew the courts from politics rather than inserting judges into the political maelstrom. Second, the implicit appeal to consensus in *Marbury* proved attractive to most early-nineteenth-century Americans, who viewed political parties with foreboding and looked back fondly upon the more nonpartisan days of the eighteenth century. Third, the doctrine of judicial review, which *Marbury* proclaimed, was not novel: many state courts already had adopted it or soon would do so. Fourth, the idea of turning to law as the protector of private property—an ideal at the core of John Marshall's jurisprudence—appealed to politically active Americans, most of whom either owned private property or expected to own it at some point in their lives.

At the heart of *Marbury v. Madison* was Chief Justice Marshall's withdrawal of the Supreme Court from partisan politics. Throughout the closing decades of eighteenth century, courts in America had been active formulators and enforcers of political policies. Judges had been active, some on the Tory but most on the Whig side, during the constitutional crisis eventuating in the War for Independence, and they remained active in the debtor-creditor and religious conflicts in various states after independence had been achieved. During the dozen years of the Washington and Adams presidencies, federal judges similarly had been active partisans of Federalist causes. President Washington had appointed only Federalists as judges, and once they had ascended the bench, they actively supported the policies of the two administrations, especially the efforts of the Adams years to repress political dissent through common-law prosecutions for seditious libel and through enforcement of the Alien and Sedition Acts. The Judiciary act of 1801 and the appointment exclusively of Federalists to the positions created under the act further injected the judiciary into the partisan strife of the preceding decade.

Arch-Federalists sought in *Marbury v. Madison* and *Stuart v. Laird* to induce the Supreme Court under Chief Justice Marshall to continue pursuing a partisan agenda. The importance of the two cases lay precisely in the possibility that the Marshall Court might have continued the earlier partisan policies of the Federalist judiciary. But, with Marshall refusing to assume a partisan posture, consensus developed, as the Republicans under Jefferson had to approve of the way the Court decided the two cases and the Federalists found themselves unable to dispute the position of the highest-ranking leaders of their party remaining in office after the defeat of President Adams in the 1800 election.

This consensus proved reassuring for most Americans after the frightful partisanship of the 1800 election and the immediately preceding years. Permanently organized political parties, as we now know them, had never been part of British or colonial political ideology during the eighteenth century, and they remained foreign to American political thinking as the nineteenth century began. Leaders of government, it was thought, should act in the interests and for the benefit of the entire citizenry, not just on behalf of those who had voted in their favor. Opposition to such disinterested leaders appeared equally inappropriate; as long as the leaders of the community were acting on behalf of all its citizens, those who opposed them had to be acting on behalf only of a few. Of course, parties and factions frequently surfaced, but they were the subjects of condemnation, not merely because of particular policies they favored but because of their very existence.

One reason Americans distrusted political factions was a fear that they would propel society into chaos and civil strife. Many Americans living in the aftermath of the election of 1800 could remember a time a quarter century earlier when political conflict had dissolved into war. Although that war had come to a glorious conclusion with Great Britain's recognition of American independence, the experience nonetheless had involved pain: loved ones had died, neighbors had gone into exile, and property had been destroyed.

There were some signs in 1800 that factional politics could again descend into civil strife. The uprising of farmers in western Massachusetts known as Shays' Rebellion was little more than a decade old, and as recently as 1795 President Washington had found it necessary to lead a contingent of armed men to put down the Whiskey Rebellion in Pennsylvania, which arose out of a refusal to pay federal excise taxes on liquor. The coercive power of the national government also had been used in 1798 against Jeffersonian editors who had attacked the policies of the Adams administration, and, partly in response to the jailing of the editors, the legislatures of Kentucky and Virginia had hinted at possible use of some vague power to nullify allegedly unconstitutional federal legislation. No one yet knew that major civil strife in America lay a distant six decades in the future, and that in the interval lay the Era of Good Feelings, when political parties would largely disappear, and the Age of Jackson, when political parties finally would be institutionalized.

Thus, when *Marbury v. Madison* used the doctrine of judicial review to curb partisan excesses and move the nation back toward its eighteenth-century tradition of consensus government, most Americans felt relieved. Almost no one objected to the case's ringing endorsement of judicial review. Later generations would find judicial review controversial, but Americans at the time of *Marbury* did not.

Although there had been some controversy about the doctrine during the 1780s, that controversy had been dissipated by the opening decade of the nineteenth century. The legitimacy of judicial review is best shown, perhaps, by its general acceptance in early-nineteenth-century state courts. By 1820, eleven of the original thirteen states were publishing reports of their cases, and the courts of ten of them had either invalidated acts of their legislatures or unequivocally asserted their right to do so. Moreover, all five of the states admitted to the Union between 1790 and 1815 had accepted judicial review by 1820, while the four states admitted between 1815 and 1819 all accepted the doctrine in cases published in the first two volumes of their reports. By 1820, in short, the principle of judicial review was, according to the 1817 Pennsylvania case of *Moore v. Houston*, "well established by the great mass of opinion, at the bar, on the bench and in the legislative assemblies of the United States."

Judicial review was so uncontroversial during the early nineteenth century in part because judges and lawyers, as they adopted the doctrine, articulated a rationale for it that was consistent with basic American political assumptions and also because courts in the first two decades of the century did not use the doctrine, as they do today, to determine conflicting issues of social policy.

The rationale for judicial review rested upon the unique American conception of sovereignty that had developed during and after the founding era debates. Americans had then rejected the traditional British view that the legislature possessed complete sovereignty, and many had begun to argue instead that sovereignty lay with the people, who by a constitution delegated limited power to the legislature. Legislators, according to the 1793 Virginia case of *Kamper v. Hawkins*, were mere "servants of the people," and a constitution, according to *Cohen v. Hoff*, an 1814 South Carolina case, "the commission from whence [they] . . . derive[d] their power." It "follow[ed]," said the Ohio Supreme Court in 1807 in *Rutherford v. M'Faddon*, "that any act in violation of the constitution, or infringing its provisions must be void, because the legislature, when they step beyond the bounds assigned them, act without authority, and their doings are no more than the doings of any other private man." The judiciary, whose duty, according to *Kamper v. Hawkins*, was "to expound *what the law is*," simply "compare[d] the legislative *act*," said *Rutherford v. M'Faddon*, "with the *constitution*." Since the constitution clearly "[could not] be adjudged void," the *Rutherford* court added that judges had no choice but to declare any "*act* which . . . [was] inconsistent with it . . . [to] be *no law*." For judges to do otherwise would be to violate their oaths and to join with the legislature in violating the constitution. Thus, judicial declarations of unconstitutionality were unavoidable and did not, according to *Federalist* Number 78, "suppose a superiority of the judicial to the legislative power," but only, as stated in an early-nineteenth-century treatise on the Constitution, "that the power of the people is superior to both."

The doctrine of judicial review, *Kamper v. Hawkins* declared, was not thought to authorize courts to "determine upon the equity, necessity, or usefulness of a law." No one doubted that courts should ignore considerations about the wisdom or expediency of a law when passing upon its validity; to weigh them, *Kamper* added, "would amount to an express interfering with the legislative branch."

Everyone agreed with Georgia's 1808 decision in *Grimball v. Ross* that courts should decide constitutional cases on the basis of "fixed principles . . . stamped with the seals of truth and authority." Their agreement was merely a corollary of an established tenet elaborated in Blackstone's *Commentaries* that judges ought not to "pronounce a new law, but to maintain and expound the old one," and, although that tenet was slowly breaking down in the early nineteenth century, people remained convinced until the 1820s that judges could draw a line between what a federal district judge in *United States v. The William* in 1808 labelled "legal discretion" and "political discretion"—between what *Federalist* Number 78 called the exercise of "*judgment*" and the "exercise [of] *will*," and between "declaring," in the language of an 1808 Virginia case, "what the law is, and . . . making a new law." Judicial review, as it developed after the 1780s, was thought, in sum, only to give the people—a single, cohesive, and indivisible body politic—protection against faithless legislators who betrayed the trust placed in them, and not to give judges authority to make law by resolving disputes between interest groups into which the people and their legislative representatives were divided.

For several decades after 1790, judges were able in cases involving judicial review to leave to legislatures the resolution of social conflicts among politically organized or identifiable interest groups and to decide only narrow questions of an apparent legal nature. During those decades, judges were rarely called upon to resolve political conflicts. Many judicial review cases, for example, were of immediate concern only to the rather small number of individuals directly involved; they decided no more than the constitutionality either of private acts granting new trials in pending litigation or of such trivial or parochial matters as the right of a sheriff to plead his recapture of an escaped debtor as a defense to a suit by a creditor, the power of the City of Philadelphia to enact a building code, and the liability of delinquent clerks to certain statutory penalties.

Other cases, like *Marbury*, while arising out of politically divisive circumstances, could be disposed of on grounds that were not divisive. A New Jersey case refusing to permit a United States senator simultaneously to hold the office of county clerk is a prime example: it raised an issue concerning which of two political factions would control an important local office, but the court was able to avoid that issue and deduce its holding from widely accepted principles of republican government that frowned upon plural officeholding. As a result, the case did not permanently favor one faction over the other or involve the judiciary in the decision of fundamental social issues underlying the factional split: it left the factions free to contest those issues in the legislative and electoral forums.

Stuart v. Laird was an example of another large category of cases. These cases, in which courts again refused to overrule legislative policy judgments, involved judicial review of statutes altering the composition, jurisdiction, or procedure of the courts. The statutes at issue typically had been passed after a campaign by radical reformers during the three decades after the Revolution to substitute popular for professional control of the legal system. Nevertheless, the statutes in large part reflected a rejection of the radical demands and a conscious policy decision by legislatures not to change the legal system fundamentally. When their constitutionality was later challenged in the courts, there was no opportunity for reconsideration of this policy decision. All the courts could do was affirm it, for their only options were either to invalidate the statutes and thereby preserve the legal system without any change or to uphold them and thereby acquiesce in the legislature's policy of minor but not fundamental change.

There were, of course, some cases in which the courts could have overturned legislation resolving divisive social conflicts between competing political interest groups. But the key fact is that between about 1790 and 1820 the judiciary did not invalidate such legislation. The relation of church and state, for example, was a prime cause of political division in Massachusetts and Virginia in the decades near the turn of the century. In both states, legislatures after a decade of debate took steps in the direction of disestablishment; in both, the courts accepted legislative policy judgments and upheld the constitutionality of the disestablishing acts.

Another social conflict that produced political divisions in many states arose from squatters placing improvements upon land they were wrongfully occupying; when the Tennessee legislature adopted an act giving squatters the right to recover the value of their improvements if the true owners sued successfully to recover the land, the Tennessee courts again accepted the legislature's resolution of the conflict and upheld the act's constitutionality. State courts also upheld other potentially sensitive legislation, such as a Georgia act postponing debt collection suits and a Pennsylvania act for regulation of the militia. And on the federal level, where the government's conduct of foreign relations had provided the chief impetus to the creation of party divisions, the lower federal courts again sustained a significant legislative decision—the Embargo Act of 1807.

The one subject on which courts invalidated significant legislation involved what we have come to know as takings cases—that is, cases in which legislators sought either to take alleged property rights from original owners and grant them to others or to limit the original owners' use rights. Chief Justice Marshall, it will be recalled, had treated *Marbury* itself as a sort of takings case: in Marshall's view a commission for office was analogous to a patent for land, and thus he regarded Madison's refusal to deliver Marbury's commission as analogous to a legislature's seizure of someone's land. If Marshall had not invalidated section 13 of the Judiciary Act and thereby held that the Supreme Court was an inappropriate forum for granting relief to Marbury, he would have protected Marbury's property in his office just as he would have protected anyone else's property in land.

Marshall continued to uphold property rights in subsequent cases. The next case in which he did so was *Fletcher v. Peck*, which involved the validity of two Georgia acts. The first act had granted land to individuals who had proceeded to sell it to others, who purchased it without notice of possible defects in the title and then subsequently passed their title to plaintiff Fletcher; the second act had repealed the first act on the ground that the first had been enacted because several state legislators had been bribed. The Court was asked to invalidate the first act because of the bribery, but Marshall declined to do so because "the principle by which judicial interference would be regulated . . . [could] not [be] clearly discerned." The validity of the first act was not properly a legal question because the Court could find no fixed, uncontroversial standards by which to resolve it.

On the other hand, Marshall readily voided the second act, because it violated "certain great principles of justice, whose authority is universally acknowledged." The issue in *Fletcher v. Peck* was, he observed, "in its nature a question of title"—more specifically, a question of legislative power to revoke a grant of land by claiming that the grant had been fraudulently obtained. According to Marshall, the law of land title was clear: "If a suit be brought to set aside a conveyance obtained by fraud, and the fraud be clearly proved, the conveyance will be set aside, as between the parties; but the rights of third persons, who are purchasers without notice, for a valuable consideration, cannot be disregarded." For the Georgia legislature to feel "itself absolved from those rules of property which are common to all the citizens of the United States, and from those principles of equity which are acknowledged in all our courts" was for it to act on the authority of "its power alone." The same power could be used to "divest any other individual of his lands, if it shall be the will of the legislature to exert it."

In sum, the Court had to invalidate one of two Georgia statutes in *Fletcher v. Peck*. It did not, however, undertake what Marshall saw as the essentially political task of identifying which of a legislator's motives for supporting a bill were legitimate. Rather, it appealed to what seemed a fixed legal principle incorporated in the contract clause of the Constitution and relied upon by the vast majority of American people: that a legislature could not take back land which it had granted away.

The most famous of the takings cases—the *Dartmouth College* case—was a variation on the same theme. It grew out of a political controversy that had roused statewide attention, but that controversy involved mere questions of patronage and personality unrelated to the legal issues on which the parties argued and the courts disposed of the case.

The dispute arose when the New Hampshire legislature attempted to revoke not a grant of land but a grant of corporate governing privileges that had been made to self-perpetuating trustees who had received land and money from other individuals. It came to the Supreme Court after a lengthy, bitter political controversy in the state. The Court voided the repeal act because it constituted a taking of vested rights protected by the contract clause. Again Marshall appealed to shared general principles to support his holding, noting that "[t]he parties in this case differ less on general principles . . . than on the application of those principles to this case." The parties agreed that "[i]f the act of incorporation be a grant of political power . . . or if the State of New Hampshire, as a government, be alone interested in its transactions, the subject [was] one in which the legislature of the State may act according to its own judgment." "But if this be a private eleemosynary institution, endowed with a capacity to take property for objects unconnected with government, whose funds are bestowed by individuals on the faith of the charter," then the legislature was restrained by the "limitation of its power imposed by the constitution of the United States." After painstakingly analyzing the facts, Marshall found Dartmouth College a private institution whose property the state accordingly could not take. This disposition of *Dartmouth College*, like the Court's disposition of *Fletcher v. Peck*, aroused little criticism from contemporaries.

Takings cases in state courts were similarly decided. For example, in the 1807 Massachusetts case of *Ellis v. Marshall*, Justice Isaac Parker, deciding the constitutionality of an act that taxed an individual for the construction of a road, distinguished between "public act[s], predicated upon a view to the general good," and "private act[s], obtained at the solicitation of individuals, for their private emolument, or for the improvement of their estates." Although he concluded that courts could not interfere with legislative evaluations of the general good, Parker invalidated the tax act because it subjected an individual "to taxation, *nolens volens*,* for the promotion of a private enterprize." Similarly, in the 1816 New York case of *Gardner v. Village of Newburgh*, Chancellor Kent voided not a tax but an uncompensated diversion of Gardner's

---

* This Latin phrase means "against his or her will."

stream by the village. Without compensation, such a taking of private property for public use was "unjust, and contrary to the first principles of government," principles "admitted by the soundest authorities, and . . . adopted by all temperate and civilized governments."

When early-nineteenth-century judges refrained from deciding highly controversial questions and merely protected vested property rights that few Americans questioned, they were not subjected to political attacks. Since most white, male Americans owned land already or expected to acquire land at some point during their lives, they did not want to see government use its takings power to challenge land titles. No organized or identifiable groups or parties had yet formed to urge use of eminent domain for redistributive purposes, and thus, when judges struck down statutes that took land without providing compensation, their decisions seemed nonpolitical. In short, the issue decided in the takings cases—the scope of state power to seize private property—was not yet a politically divisive one, but one for which judges could find answers by reference to broadly shared beliefs about the nature of republican government.

Thus, as one surveys the cases between about 1790 and 1820 involving claims that state statutes violated state constitutions or that federal statutes violated the federal Constitution, a persistent pattern emerges. The pattern discloses that the courts by 1820 had begun to hold legislation unconstitutional with some frequency, but that their working understanding of the scope of their constitutional activity was sufficiently different from ours that, although we term their activity judicial review, we must not lose sight of the difference.

Early-nineteenth-century courts, unlike our own, still sought to leave, and in fact succeeded in leaving, to legislatures the resolution of conflicts between organized social interest groups. Once a legislature had resolved a conflict in a manner having widespread public support, judges would in practice view the resolution as that of the people at large, even though one or more organized groups continued to oppose it, and would give it conclusive effect, at least as long as a finding of inconsistency with the constitution was not plain and unavoidable. Judges of the early nineteenth century such as John Marshall, unlike judges of today, did not see judicial review as a mechanism for protecting minority rights against majoritarian infringement.

Early judicial review thus rested upon a perception of political reality that differed sharply from current perceptions. Judges of the early nineteenth century viewed "the people" as a politically homogeneous and cohesive body possessing common political goals and aspirations, not as a congeries of factions and interest groups, each having its own set of goals and aspirations. The concern of judges in early constitutional cases was with the potentiality of conflict between legislators and their constituents—with the possibility that faithless legislators might betray the trust placed in them by the people. The perceived purpose of judicial review was to protect the people from such possible betrayals, not to impose obstacles in the path of decisions made by the people's agents in due execution of their trust. As a result, little popular objection arose either to the doctrine of judicial review or to the leading Supreme Court case, *Marbury v. Madison*, that had proclaimed it.

But the political consensus underlying the early-nineteenth-century practice of judicial review could not endure. As the circle of politically active Americans expanded during the course of the century, constitutional principles, especially principles about the sanctity of private property, became the subject of political debate. As a result, some new foundation for judicial review was needed. In the next chapter we shall examine how, at the very time judicial review was becoming established as a fixture of the American constitutional system, its Marshallian foundations were eroded. Then we shall turn in future chapters to the process in the twentieth century by which new foundations for the practice were articulated, both in America and ultimately around the world.

CHAPTER 6

Judicial Review Becomes
Politically Charged

As we have just seen, neither the doctrine of judicial review nor the cases decided pursuant to the doctrine aroused significant controversy during the three decades from 1790 to 1820, in the midst of which *Marbury v. Madison* was decided. Like Chief Justice Marshall, many judges avoided conflict with legislatures over controversial issues of political or social import. Statutes that were declared unconstitutional, like the section of the Judiciary Act of 1789 invalidated in the *Marbury* case, typically involved narrow issues of judicial jurisdiction and procedure of little interest to any larger political public. Even cases passing upon the power of legislatures to seize and regulate property aroused little controversy since nearly all politically active Americans owned property and applauded judicial attempts to protect private rights from legislative infringement.

Judicial review also was noncontroversial in the early nineteenth century because courts exercised the function only on rare occasions. After declaring section 13 of the 1789 Judiciary Act unconstitutional in *Marbury v. Madison*, the Supreme Court did not invalidate another act of Congress for fifty-four years. State courts similarly were far less active in striking down state legislation in the early part of the nineteenth century than they would be in the later part.

Like the Supreme Court of the United States, the Supreme Court of Indiana held only two legislative acts unconstitutional prior to 1850, while the Supreme Judicial Court of Massachusetts struck down only ten state statutes before 1860. The highest court of Virginia invalidated only four laws prior to 1860. Courts were most active in judicial review cases in New York, but even there few statutes were invalidated prior to 1850, at least in comparison with the number declared unconstitutional after 1850; only ten statutes were held void prior to 1840, and only eighteen were invalidated between 1841 and 1850.

There was only one case in the first half of the nineteenth century, *Eakin v. Raub*, in which controversy over the doctrine of judicial review materialized. In *Eakin*, Pennsylvania's Judge John Banister Gibson authored a dissenting opinion advocating abandonment of judicial review. Gibson recited all the common arguments against the doctrine. He noted that "repugnance to the constitution is not always self-evident" and that, since people "seldom . . . think exactly alike," "conflicts" in interpreting constitutional provisions would be "inevitable." If the judiciary once entered into considerations of unconstitutionality, he wondered, "where shall it stop."

For Gibson, in short, there were no clear lines, particularly since review of the constitutionality of legislation required judges to make what he labeled "political," as distinguished from "civil" or legal, determinations. He further argued that the legislature possessed "pre-eminence" in government; "the power of the legislature," according to Gibson, is "the power of the people, and sovereign as far as it extends." Gibson simply could see no basis for courts to question political decisions made by the people; for him, judicial review denied "a *postulate* in the theory of our government, and the very basis of the superstructure, that the people are wise, virtuous, and competent to manage their own affairs."

Ultimately, though, in the 1830s, 1840s, and 1850s, Gibson's views were rejected, and judges in their opinions began to articulate new justifications for judicial review. One justification was the weight of precedent: by 1860 courts had held legislation unconstitutional in over 150 cases. As one North Carolina judge observed in 1861 in the case of *Barnes v. Barnes*, "[t]he right, and the duty of this Court, to give judgment on the constitutional power of the Legislature in making statutes, . . . [has been] established by so many elaborated opinions of this Court, and of the Supreme Court of the United States, and of our sister States, as to make a further discussion or citation of authorities a useless attempt at a display of learning." Courts, according to the 1848 Georgia case of *Flint River Steamboat Co. v. Foster*, would "not stop, at [that] late day, to inquire" into "their duty to declare Acts of the Legislature, repugnant to the Constitution, void," for while "[t]hese grave questions once elicited much discussion," the matter now seemed settled; as the New York Court of Appeals declared in the leading 1856 case of *Wynehamer v. People*, "[t]he right of courts to declare legislative enactments, in derogation of the constitution, void . . . [had] been too long and steadily exercised in this country to be now doubted or questioned."

Indeed, even Judge Gibson felt compelled by 1845 to recant his former views, in part because of the weight of authority favoring judicial review and the apparent acquiescence of the people therein. In the 1845 case of *Norris v. Clymer*, Gibson announced that he now had come to favor judicial review "from experience of the necessity of the case." "Experience [had] prove[d]" to Gibson that the constitution was "thoughtlessly but habitually violated." Other judges agreed. In *De Chastellux v. Fairchild*, the Pennsylvania Supreme Court observed again in 1850 that "[g]reat wrongs may undoubtedly be perpetrated by legislative bodies," which "from mistaken views of policy," in the language of the Michigan case of *People v. Gallagher* some six years later, often passed legislation "greatly injurious to the best interests of the State, or . . . oppressive in its operation on one class of citizens." One New York trial judge in an 1848 case, for example, thought "*excessive legislation* . . . [to be] the great legal curse of the age . . . drawing every thing within its grasp," while California and Indiana judges, in *People ex rel. Attorney General v. Burbank* in 1859 and in *Beebe v. State* in 1855, respectively, found their "statute book[s] . . . replete with crude and unconstitutional legislation" and other "very odious enactment[s]."

By the middle of the nineteenth century, in short, judicial review had become an accepted feature of American law. The public had acquiesced in it, and no one doubted that judges had jurisdiction to declare legislative acts unconstitutional and void. Indeed, the doctrine of judicial review had become so firmly established that no one could any longer question its propriety. With the doctrine firmly established, judges began to exercise their power of review with greater frequency, and they also began to use the power in a fashion that involved them in substantial controversy.

A marked change occurred in the frequency of cases invalidating legislation. Although the United States Supreme Court had declared only 2 acts of Congress void prior to 1860, it held 21 unconstitutional between 1865 and 1898. Similarly, the number of instances in which state courts held state legislation unconstitutional rose to 31 between 1860 and 1893 in Massachusetts, to 40 between 1861 and 1902 in Virginia, to 94 between 1850 and 1899 in Indiana, and to 266 between 1851 and 1900 in New York. The Ohio Supreme Court was also very active in the 1880s and 1890s, as it struck down 57 legislative acts, while in Minnesota, approximately 70 statutes were held void between 1885 and 1899.

Not only did growth occur in the number of instances of judicial review; the second half of the nineteenth century also witnessed an increase in the controversial nature of many of the issues on which judges passed. The trend began in the late 1850s with two cases in leading courts—the Supreme Court of the United States and the Court of Appeals of New York. The two cases were *Scott v. Sandford* and *Wynehamer v. People*, in both of which the courts acted, as their predecessors had earlier in the century, to protect private property rights. But in both cases, protection of property clashed with powerful reform movements—namely, antislavery and temperance, and, as a result, the judiciary's protection of property rights was not received with the same equanimity as the public in earlier decades had received it.

The *Dred Scott* case, which was decided in 1857, involved two issues. The first was whether the federal court in which Scott had commenced his case had jurisdiction. Scott's claim of jurisdiction was predicated upon diversity of citizenship: Scott claimed to be a citizen of Missouri, while the defendant, John Sandford, was a citizen of New York. Sandford responded, however, and the Supreme Court ruled, that African Americans could not be citizens and hence could not maintain suits such as the one brought by Dred Scott in federal courts. This jurisdictional finding would have been an adequate basis for dismissing Scott's claim and declining to pass on its merits, but the Court did not rest its holding on lack of jurisdiction alone and proceeded to the second issue raised by Scott—his claim of freedom.

Scott had based his claim, at least in part, on the fact that a previous master had taken him to reside at Fort Snelling, then in the Territory of Upper Louisiana and now in Minnesota, which Congress in the Missouri Compromise of 1820 had declared to be free territory. The Supreme Court answered this claim by declaring the Missouri Compromise unconstitutional. Rejecting the argument that the provision in the Northwest Ordinance of 1787 prohibiting slavery provided a precedent for congressional prohibition of slavery in other territories, the Court held that Congress had a constitutional obligation to keep all territories open for settlement and development by citizens of all states, including slaveowners, and that fulfillment of that obligation necessitated protection of the property of citizens, including their property in slaves.

This decision infuriated antislavery proponents. Although it was no longer possible to claim that the Supreme Court lacked authority to declare acts of Congress unconstitutional, antislavery leaders frequently maintained that the Court's holding would not bar Congress from enacting and enforcing future antislavery legislation, subject to review by future Supreme Courts. Moreover, they argued that the Court had erred in declaring the Missouri Compromise unconstitutional. According to an 1857 report to the New York legislature, the invalidation of the Missouri Compromise was "contrary to the fundamental principle . . . that every man has an inalienable right to his liberty, and that it can only be taken from him by a statute of the State in which he lives." Liberty, according to the advocates of antislavery, was the natural state of man, whereas slavery—that is, property in man—could occur only when local police regulations altered that natural state. For the forces of antislavery, which would soon capture control of Congress and the presidency in the 1860 elections, the Supreme Court got it backward when it protected property rather than liberty from legislative regulation and encroachment.

A year earlier, in 1856, the Court of Appeals of New York had decided another controversial case, *Wynehamer v. People*. *Wynehamer* reflected a clash between property rights and temperance advocates who were striving to purify society by forbidding consumption of alcoholic beverages. The narrow issue presented to the Court was whether state legislation prohibiting the sale of alcoholic beverages could be applied to liquors owned by individuals before passage of the act; the Court of Appeals concluded that the owners had a vested property right and that legislation interfering with that right was therefore unconstitutional.

As had been true in the aftermath of *Dred Scott*, little question arose concerning the power of judicial review; as one judge declared, "[t]he right of courts to declare legislative enactments, in derogation of the constitution, void . . . [had] been too long and steadily exercised in this country to be now doubted or questioned." The controversy was about the substantive issue in the case—whether to protect alleged private rights of property or to promote the perfectionist scheme of temperance advocates. Whatever decision it reached, the court would disappoint a powerful political group; as one judge wrote, that "danger" arose "when[ever] theories, alleged to be founded in natural reason or inalienable rights, but subversive of the just and necessary powers of government, attract[ed] the belief of considerable classes of men."

In the last third of the nineteenth century, judges continued to confront cases in which claims of property rights and individual economic liberty stood in opposition to reform programs of powerful political groups. In the United States Supreme Court, the two most important cases were *Munn v. Illinois* and *Pollock v. Farmers' Loan & Trust Co.*

In *Munn*, the Court upheld the Granger laws that had been enacted by the Illinois legislature at the behest of farmers and their political allies for the purpose of regulating railroads and grain dealers. The specific statute at issue regulated the prices charged by warehouses in the city of Chicago, the owners of which claimed that, as holders of private property, they were immune from legislative regulation. The Supreme Court did not question the starting proposition that private property owners were exempt from regulation, but it did hold that, since the warehouses were affected with a public interest, the claim of their owners to immunity was lost. *Munn* was like *Marbury*, in that the Court avoided a direct, head-on conflict with a powerful legislative majority, but it also was unlike *Marbury*, in that it involved a major social controversy pitting a majoritarian legislature against private individuals seeking to resist legislative power.

Pollock v. Farmers' Loan & Trust Co. again pitted a majoritarian legislature—in this instance, the Congress of the United States—against private wealth holders. In *Pollock*, the Supreme Court not only failed to avoid, but indeed exacerbated, the confrontation by declaring the federal income tax unconstitutional, in part on the ground that its progressive rate structure resulted in unequal taxation. The crisis generated by *Pollock* was resolved only when Congress proposed and three-fourths of the states ratified what is arguably the most significant provision of the Constitution—the Sixteenth Amendment, which made the constitutionality of an income tax unquestionable.

Analogous cases pitting property and other individual economic rights against legislative regulatory power occurred during the closing decades of the nineteenth century in the state courts. Arising out of the same social conflict as *Wynehammer v. People* was *McCullough v. Brown*, where the Supreme Court of South Carolina declared unconstitutional an act that gave the state a monopoly of the liquor trade; the court thought the state monopoly would interfere with the liberty of individuals to enter the trade for themselves.

Other state cases saw legislative efforts to improve working conditions of laborers founder on the rocks of economic liberty. Thus, in New York, the 1885 case of *Matter of Jacobs* struck down legislation prohibiting the manufacture of cigars in tenement houses unless certain health and safety regulations were satisfied. In Pennsylvania, *Godcharles v. Wigeman*, decided in 1886, invalidated an act requiring mining and manufacturing companies to pay wages only in currency, while an 1893 case, *State v. Loomis*, held the similar Missouri "scrip" act unconstitutional. Analogous legislation, requiring corporations to pay wages on a weekly basis, was invalidated by the Illinois Supreme Court in 1893 in *Braceville Coal Co. v. People.*

In deciding in these cases to protect property rights and individual economic liberty at the expense of those who were using legislative power to promote their vision of a just and good society, judges were seen by progressive reformers to be engaging in a fundamentally different activity than that in which John Marshall had engaged when his Court, early in the nineteenth century, had commenced the judiciary's protection of property. Marshall had restricted judicial review mainly to cases in which statutes could be invalidated on the basis of a widely shared consensus about the limitations of legislative power. He had conceptualized judicial review as a mechanism for protecting the public at large against faithless legislators. Aware that they lacked power to coerce acceptance of their judgments, Marshall and his contemporaries on the bench rarely attempted to impose the views of one segment of society upon another. Theirs was a quaint conception of judicial review, quite unlike the conception with which we today are familiar.

By the latter part of the nineteenth century, however, judicial review had begun to take on a more modern look. It was beginning to be seen not as a device for protecting the people against their government, but as a protection for minorities against majorities.

Long before the mid-nineteenth century, it was axiomatic, in the words of one delegate to the 1821 New York constitutional convention, that the function of politics was "to secure to the majority of the people that control and influence in every section of the state to which they are justly entitled." Yet political majoritarianism raised difficulties. Courts well knew, as stated in the 1850 Pennsylvania case of *De Chastellux v. Fairchild*, that legislatures concerned only with the interests of the majority would willingly sanction "the sacrifice of individual right" since individual rights were "too remotely connected with the objects and contests of the masses to attract their attention." Minorities, that is, could not protect themselves in the legislative process. As another Pennsylvania judge explained in 1851 in *Ervine's Appeal:*

[W]hen, in the exercise of proper legislative powers, general laws are enacted, which bear or may bear on the whole community, if they are unjust and against the spirit of the constitution, the whole community will be interested to procure their repeal by a voice potential. And that is the great security for just and fair legislation.

But when individuals are selected from the mass, and laws are enacted affecting their property, without summons or notice, at the instigation of an interested party, who is to stand up for them, thus isolated from the mass, in injury and injustice, or where are they to seek relief from such acts of despotic power?

The judge answered his question by granting to minorities a "refuge . . . in the courts, the only secure place for determining conflicting rights by due course of law." Without such refuge, the Michigan Supreme Court declared in 1856 in *People v. Gallagher*, minorities would "stand in no better attitude, irrespective of the fundamental principles and maxims of free government, than that of the most abject slaves to the majority." Indeed, the Ohio Supreme Court expressed its fear in the 1851 case of *Griffith v. Commissioners* that "if the rights of *minorities* . . . [were] not observed, it . . . [would] not be long before the *majorities* . . . [themselves would] be in bondage."

Thus, by the 1850s, the courts had articulated a new theoretical justification for judicial review: that it was needed, according to an 1831 Tennessee case, "to secure to weak and unpopular minorities and individuals, equal rights with the majority"; according to an 1836 case, also in Tennessee, "to prevent majorities in times of high political excitement from passing partial laws"; and according to an 1851 New York case, to protect "minorities against the caprices, recklessness, or prejudices of majorities." Or as one Virginia judge had summarized the theory in *Goddin v. Crump* as early as 1837:

It must be admitted that at the institution of civil government founded on the rights of all, the will of the majority must prevail over the opinions and interests of the minority: but when such government is established, its great object is to protect the rights of the minority from the tyranny of the majority; a tyranny more inflexible and implacable than the tyranny of a single despot. . . . To effect this relief against the tyranny of majorities, written constitutions were devised by the American people.

By the middle of the nineteenth century, in short, judicial review had become reestablished on a new basis—the basis on which it would function in *Scott v. Sandford* and *Pollock v. Farmers' Loan & Trust Co.* and in numerous twentieth-century cases. No longer a device for protecting the people as a whole from faithless legislators, judicial review had become a means for sectional and political minorities or individuals lacking control of the legislative process to obtain reconsideration of the legislature's decisions and overturn the legislature's political judgments. It had become a vehicle through which judges could keep the nation loyal to what they thought were the fundamental precepts of American life. Contrary to its original conception, judicial review, as the Indiana Court proclaimed in *Beebe v. State* in 1851, had become a mechanism for the courts "to protect the people against themselves."

But judicial review in the late nineteenth century still had not assumed what would become its late-twentieth-century form. Judicial review had not yet come to protect the interests of powerless minorities identified on racial, ethnic, religious, or sexual grounds. On the contrary, its purpose, according to Christopher Tiedeman's 1886 *Treatise on the Limitations of the Police Power*, was to protect the most powerful of minorities—the rich—against "[g]overnmental interference," which was

demanded everywhere as a sufficient panacea for every social evil which threatens the prosperity of society. Socialism, Communism, and Anarchism are rampant throughout the civilized world. The State is called on to protect the weak against the shrewdness of the stronger, to determine what wages a workman shall receive for his labor, and how many hours daily he shall labor. . . .

Contemplating these extraordinary demands of the great

army of discontents, and their apparent power, with the growth and development of universal suffrage, to enforce their views of civil polity upon the civilized world, the conservative classes stand in constant fear of the advent of an absolutism more tyrannical and more unreasoning than any before experienced by man, the absolutism of a democratic majority.

In short, judicial review had emerged, Tiedeman continued, as the means "to protect private rights against the radical experimentation of social reformers . . . in the cause of social order." From the perspective of progressive reformers and historians who, in the early decades of the twentieth century, would author the first histories of judicial review, protecting private property against regulatory legislation involved policy choice and judicial intrusion into the domain of politics. For reasons about to be examined, however, conservative lawyers and their judicial supporters could still understand themselves to be acting in a legal capacity in property rights cases.

CHAPTER 7

The Judiciary as Protector of Minorities

The crux of the original decision in *Marbury v. Madison*, as we have seen, was John Marshall's distinction between law and politics. Law dealt with those matters as to which there existed substantial community acquiescence in response to which juries could render unanimous verdicts and courts generally could expect compliance with their mandates. Politics, in contrast, involved questions about which the nation, the states, and local communities were divided. In connection with those questions, judges could not expect randomly chosen juries routinely to reach unanimous verdicts, nor could judges themselves have a basis for deciding to accept the views of one political faction rather than the views of another. All courts could do was place their trust in the majoritarian electoral process and defer to the decisions of elected legislatures and executive officials.

For more than a century after the *Marbury* case was handed down, conservative jurists were able largely to maintain Marshall's distinction between law and politics and to understand that they were enforcing legal rights rather than making political decisions when they held acts of the coordinate, legislative branch unconstitutional. Thus, we have seen how at the time of *Marbury* and for several decades thereafter, judges routinely refrained from entering the political thicket and applied the doctrine of judicial review mainly to issues of narrow scope that aroused little political interest or controversy. Usually, courts were able to apply the doctrine of judicial review only to statutes that legislators had passed in betrayal of the trust reposed by their constituents, and thereby the courts were able to appear to be upholding the will of the people against their faithless agents.

On occasion, of course, judges trespassed upon the political domain, as in the 1857 Supreme Court decision of *Scott v. Sandford*, which declared the Missouri Compromise of 1820 unconstitutional and held that slaveowners could maintain their property in slaves in any territory of the United States. But on those occasions, political leaders who disagreed with the courts' results criticized their decisions, campaigned against them, and ultimately ignored them. In the aftermath of the *Dred Scott* case, for example, leaders of the Republican Party turned the Supreme Court's holding into a contentious issue in the 1858 and 1860 elections, and when they gained majorities in Congress in 1861, they promptly enacted and enforced legislation prohibiting slavery in the territories, despite the fact that the Court in *Dred Scott* had declared such laws unconstitutional.

When courts in the *Marbury* era initially began striking down legislative infringements of private property rights, they were again acting in support of a legal consensus on which the public as a whole agreed. Even when, in the late nineteenth century, the scope of legislative power over private property became a more contentious issue, judges could still understand that they were enforcing legal rights against legislative power. They could understand, in the closing decades of the century, that they had been protecting property from legislative infringement for several decades, and in many cases they merely had to follow precedent in order to continue providing protection. Moreover, although the distribution of wealth was becoming increasingly unequal, most voters still owned or expected to own property and therefore remained committed to a legal regime of private property rights. Thus, late-nineteenth- and early-twentieth-century judges could and often did invalidate legislation affecting private property on the ground that it responded to the demands of special interests and violated longstanding, fundamental norms of the American polity.

The notion that judicial review merely protected legal rights rather than adjudicating political controversies collapsed, however, in the late 1930s. Beginning in those years, the line between law and politics grew increasingly blurred, as judges began to trespass more and more frequently upon domains they had previously left to the democratic political process. The underlying cause was a growing loss of faith in that process.

By the 1930s, popular government and the institutions of mass democracy had become problematic. Manipulations of mass politics in that and recent decades had put Hitler and Mussolini into power in Germany and Italy, transformed Senator Huey Long and Father Charles Coughlin into national figures famed for their opposition to President Franklin D. Roosevelt's New Deal, and led to mass oppression of minorities in Germany and the American South. As what the Reverend Dr. Raymond C. Knox, chaplain of Columbia University, labelled the "shadow of the swastika" spread across Europe in the final years of the 1930s, American thinkers such as the chaplain grew concerned about the "menace to . . . freedom" that it posed and urged "all creeds to unite against" what Congressman Vito Mercantonio in 1938 called "that canker of fascism and Nazism" in order to preserve what John Maynard Keynes had earlier called "liberty of thought and criticism." "The rise of totalitarianism," according to the renowned theologian Reinhold Niebuhr, prompted Americans in the closing years of the 1930s "to view all collectivist answers . . . with increased apprehension" and to recognize that "a too powerful state is dangerous to our liberties."

Alarm about the spread of totalitarianism overlapped emerging concerns about interest-group politics—concerns that undercut classical arguments in defense of majoritarian democracy. Supporters of democracy had long argued that if the majority of the people were left free to elect their leaders, the government that resulted would mirror the common will of the people and accordingly would pursue the public good. The realization that the people aligned themselves into interest groups, on the other hand, proved corrosive of the very ideas of common will and public good. In a political culture of interest-group politics, legislation came to appear as favoritism toward some groups at the expense of the freedom and equality of other groups. Judicial review, in turn, no longer appeared as an effort of judges to uphold the law against faithless legislators but as a judicial choice to favor particular interests in the polity against other interests.

Judge Learned Hand was one of the first to elaborate a vision of interest-group politics. In a 1928 speech before the American Law Institute, he observed:

> Sometimes . . . we speak of the judges as representing a common-will. . . . [But] they are not charged with power to decide the major conflicts. . . . We think of the legislature as the place for resolving these, and so indeed it is. But if we go further and insist that there at any rate we have an expression of a common-will, . . . we should be wrong again. I will not of course deny that there are statutes of which we can say that they carry something like the assent of a majority. But most legislation is not of that kind; it represents the insistence of a compact and formidable minority.

Two years later a conservative law professor at the University of Pennsylvania, John Dickinson, embellished Hand's earlier insight:

> The task of government . . . is not to express an imaginary popular will, but to effect adjustments among the various special wills and purposes which at any given time are pressing for realization. . . . Government, from this point of view, is primarily an arbitrator, and since practically every arbitration must result in giving to one side more of what it thinks it ought to have than the other side is willing to admit, every governmental act can be viewed as favoring in some degree some particular and partial "will," or special interest.

As events unfolded through the 1930s, even New Dealers began to abandon President Roosevelt's early rhetoric, which had viewed the masses as "part and parcel of a rounded whole" who understood that "we all go up, or else we all go down, as one people" and "that the welfare of your family or mine cannot be bought at the sacrifice of our neighbor's family." By the late 1930s, at least some New Dealers had learned from experience that the people were divided into special interests. Accordingly they had begun to perceive a need for the enactment of laws designed to promote the organization of economically weak groups so that they might hold their own against stronger rivals.

This development pointed, in turn, toward a redefinition of democracy. As political scientist John Chamberlain wrote in a 1940 book, a democratic "society" was one in which "various groups and classes" whose "power [was] evenly spread," faced each other with "economic checks and balances to parallel the political checks and balances," all of which produced "a state of tension . . . that permit[ted] no one group to dare bid for the total power." Over the next three decades, this view was codified in such classics as V. O. Key's *Politics, Parties, & Pressure Groups*, Douglass Adair's 1951 article rescuing Madison's theory of factions in *Federalist* Number 10 from the dustbin of history, and Theodore Lowi's *The End of Liberalism*.

No one better captured the change that occurred in American political ideology as a result of the emergence of interest-groups at home and fascism and Nazism abroad than the New Deal senator, Robert F. Wagner. In a 1938 speech, Wagner declared:

As we reflect sorrowfully on the turn in world events . . . , we pose in our own minds the essential governmental problem of our times. In the 18th and 19th centuries, that problem was how to establish the will of the majority in representative government. In the world of today, the problem is how to protect the integrity and civil liberties of minority races and groups. The humane solution of that problem is now the supreme test of democratic principles, the test indeed, of civilized government.

We in America have long cherished the picture of a great melting pot. . . . That picture, we must all admit, is marred in this State . . . by certain manifestations of racial intolerance and prejudice. . . . The bestial manifestations of anti-Semitism abroad are happily absent from our national scene. We cannot, however, be blind to the forms of anti-Semitism prevalent at home. These manifestations have been vigorously challenged by spokesmen of all creeds, and many notorious instances have met with effective protest.

Far less effective in marshaling informed public opinion and suffering from discrimination and prejudice so deep-seated as to be taken for granted by the community at large, are the half million Negroes in the State.

After describing graphically the discrimination that victimized African Americans in New York in the 1930s, Wagner concluded:

In the final analysis the so-called Negro problem, or any other minority problem, is but another aspect of man's eternal struggle for freedom and justice, a problem that solves itself when democracy is extended into every phase of our material life.

Few other thinkers as early as 1938 had seen the future as clearly as did Wagner in this speech. At that time, many still believed that the essential issue for government was how to establish the will of the majority of the people. In the world of today, however, the issue surely has become how to end racial, ethnic, and religious intolerance and to protect the integrity and civil liberties of minority races and groups.

Our task is to comprehend the significance for judges and judicial review of this change in the understanding of the essential task of just government. We need to grasp how judicial review changed after the late 1930s. Only then can we fully appreciate how *Marbury v. Madison* was the precursor for, yet distinct from, the judicial review that exists in America and the world today.

In a government charged with the task of effectuating the will of the majority, judicial review has a necessarily small role. As the least democratic branch of government, judges have little basis on which to outguess legislators as to the content of the majority's will. Nor should they attempt to thwart that will. Thus, they can invalidate legislation only to protect the people from the occasionally faithless legislature that has abused its trust or to secure rights that the people in drafting the Constitution had placed outside the jurisdiction of the majoritarian political process.

But if the essential task of just government is to protect the liberty and equality of minorities from an overbearing majority, then undemocratic judges have a special role to play, and their exercise of the power of judicial review of legislation becomes a main instrument of just government. Democratically elected legislators and elected executive officials, who are responsible to popular majorities, cannot be trusted to protect minorities from those majorities. Judges with life tenure can be.

Supreme Court Justice Harlan Fiske Stone came to this realization in the same year that Senator Wagner articulated his new understanding of the essential duty of just government. The timing was not coincidental; both men were responding to the same forces of injustice that they observed spreading in the world. As Stone wrote in a 1938 letter to Judge Irving Lehman of the New York Court of Appeals, he had become "deeply concerned about the increasing racial and religious intolerance which seem[ed] to bedevil the world" and which might "be augmented in this country." For this reason, he had thought it necessary to draft what has since become one of American constitutional law's most important texts—footnote 4 of *United States v. Carolene Products Co.* The footnote announced that the Court would scrutinize strictly legislation "directed at particular religious, . . . or national, . . . or racial minorities" when "prejudice against discrete and insular minorities may be a special condition, which tends seriously to curtail the operation of those political processes ordinarily to be relied upon to protect minorities." On such occasions, a "correspondingly more searching judicial inquiry" was required to guarantee the fairness, legality, and justice of a majoritarian act.

The Supreme Court's new understanding of the nature and function of judicial review transformed the practice within a few years. In 1938, the same year that Justice Stone wrote *Carolene Products*, the Court decided the first in a line of cases in which it struck down segregation in educational contexts; the line of cases culminated sixteen years later in *Brown v. Board of Education*. Four years after footnote 4, the Court handed down its first decision in *Williams v. North Carolina*, which came to the assistance of a then unpopular minority—spouses seeking divorce—and invalidated much state legislative and decisional law placing obstacles in the path of enforcing divorce decrees from jurisdictions other than the state in which a spouse seeking a divorce resided or had married.

The next year, in *West Virginia State Board of Education v. Barnette*, the Court protected the small sect of Jehovah's Witnesses against a popular, majoritarian requirement that they salute the flag—an act deemed sinful pursuant to their religious beliefs. After initial decisions to the contrary, the Court began in the late 1950s to uphold the free speech rights of Communists and other political dissidents. Footnote 4 of *Carolene Products* arguably came to its fullest fruition in the 1960s and early 1970s, when the Warren Court and its successor, the early Burger Court, reapportioned Congress and the state legislatures, outlawed prayer in the public schools, upheld the procedural rights of criminal defendants, and guaranteed many aspects of sexual privacy. In all these cases, the Court came to the defense of unpopular, suspect minorities and invalidated laws with which the vast majority of Americans agreed.

Of course, the Supreme Court has not always upheld minority rights in the years since 1938. More often than not, it has upheld popular laws adopted through the majoritarian political process despite their negative impact on minorities. And as the Court has vacillated in its judgments about the constitutionality of statutes, sometimes deciding in favor of the interests of minorities and sometimes deciding against them, it has routinely made judgments about the desirability of particular social policies.

Moreover, the Court has been criticized for making case-by-case policy judgments, and the pull of *Marbury*'s distinction between law and politics has been so strong that the Court has continued to strive earnestly to find legalistic grounds for its decisions, independent of the will of political and judicial actors. Justices and students of the Court have argued that the Court should enforce minority rights only if those rights have a basis in the Constitution's text or alternatively that in deciding cases, the Court should protect political processes that render government more responsive to genuine majority demands. Others have urged the Court to follow rules of law said to be implicit in the governmental structure established by the Constitution, while still others have urged the Court to derive rules of law from philosophical first principles, whether Kantian or utilitarian. Each of these approaches, it is said, will provide the Supreme Court with fixed legal principles with which to decide cases and will make recourse to ad hoc policy determination unnecessary.

Unfortunately, none of these approaches adequately balances minority rights against majoritarian power. The Founding Fathers did not draft the text of the Constitution with a purpose of securing minority rights as their main goal, nor was the structure of the Constitution designed for that purpose. Kantian and utilitarian philosophy similarly do not have the protection of minorities as their chief ends. Protecting discrete and insular racial, ethnic, and religious minorities is a mid-twentieth-century idea, not an eighteenth- or nineteenth-century one. Of course, decisions, such as those reapportioning legislatures, that are designed to enable majorities among the people to influence legislative decision making more effectively also will not aid minorities in the protection of their rights.

Ultimately, the critics of the Court are misguided in expecting the justices to decide judicial review cases involving racial, religious, or cultural minorities without making repeated, ad hoc policy judgments. The need for such judgments follows almost ineluctably from the suggestion of Senator Wagner that the essential task of government in our times is not to establish the will of the majority but to protect the integrity and civil liberties of minorities. Legislative majorities are too self-interested to be trusted with that task: some other institution of government is needed. Because of its independence and impartiality, the judiciary appears the most promising alternative. But no one has promulgated clear legal principles that can direct judges in the performance of the task. Their job is not to champion the interests of minorities on all occasions, but only when it is fair and just to do so. And in the absence of clear rules, they can only decide what is fair and just by recourse to their intuitions about sound social policy.

CHAPTER 8

The Worldwide Spread of Judicial Review

Until the twentieth century, *Marbury v. Madison* and judicial review of the constitutionality of acts of coordinate legislative bodies were mainly American phenomena. Of course, there were imperial and federal systems in which courts at the central capital determined the validity of legislation that had been adopted at the periphery. The United States itself was such a federal system, in which the Supreme Court routinely decided whether state laws were consistent with federal law and the federal Constitution. By the 1930s the British Privy Council likewise had developed into a judicial body that passed upon the validity of laws adopted in the British Commonwealth's dominions and in Britain's colonies. But the United States was the only major nation in which a judicial body, the Supreme Court, adjudicated the constitutionality of acts of a coordinate legislative body, Congress. Most notably, the Privy Council never addressed the validity of legislation adopted by what everyone understood to be its superior, the Westminster Parliament.

Prior to 1920, only a few other nations, nearly all in Latin America, had adopted judicial review. Argentina, Brazil, Columbia, Mexico, Venezuela, and even small nations like the Dominican Republic, among others, fell under the influence of United States constitutional ideas in the mid-nineteenth century and incorporated variants of *Marbury v. Madison* into their constitutional systems. Alexis de Tocqueville's *Democracy in America*, which emphasized the central role of judges in American politics, played a fundamental role in this transfer of judicial review to other Western Hemisphere nations.

Movement in the direction of embracing judicial review began occurring in Europe in the aftermath of World War I, as the defeated Central Powers adopted and administered new constitutions. The first European nation to adopt any form of judicial review following the war was Czechoslovakia, although the Constitutional Tribunal created by its 1920 constitution never developed effective jurisdiction over claims of unconstitutionality and disappeared in 1938. Of greater significance was the tribunal established by the Austrian constitution of 1920, under the guidance of Austria's leading jurisprudential figure, Professor Hans Kelsen, who also served as a member of the constitutional court until 1929. The 1920 Austrian constitution expressly established the principle of its own supremacy and conferred jurisdiction on the Constitutional Tribunal to declare invalid any inconsistent legislation.

Nonetheless, prior to the reinstitution of judicial review following the separation of Austria from Germany in 1945 and to constitutional reforms in 1975, the Austrian variant of judicial review was a insipid replica of the vibrant American practice. The key limitations in Austria resulted from procedural restrictions, pursuant to which only specific judicial and other governmental institutions, within three years after the passage of any statute, were authorized to challenge its constitutionality. If proceedings were not commenced by appropriate officials within the appropriate time frame, the validity of a statute no longer could be challenged.

Something more analogous to *Marbury v. Madison* occurred in Weimar Germany. The 1919 Weimar Constitution created a Tribunal of State Justice, with jurisdiction over constitutional disputes between two or more *Lander*, or states, or between the national government and a *Land*. It was also empowered to try allegations that the president, the chancellor, or any minister had violated the constitution. In addition, the Tribunal of the Reich, the highest court in the ordinary judiciary, received jurisdiction to adjudicate the compatability of legislation enacted by the *Lander* with imperial legislation. These provisions left a gap, however: no institution was charged with determining the compatability of imperial legislation with the imperial constitution. In language akin to that of John Marshall in *Marbury*, the Tribunal of the

Reich declared in a 1925 decision that "the submission of the judge to the law" implied "the power of the judge to question the validity of statutes of the Empire . . . when they are in opposition to other preeminent dispositions that must be observed by the judge," notably "the Imperial Constitution."

But this decision was heavily criticized, and thus the place of judicial review in German law remained unclear up to 1933, when Hitler came to power. It is noteworthy that no one sought to employ the doctrine to protect individual rights against Nazi atrocities. With Hitler's rise to power and Germany's subsequent subjugation of Austria and Czechoslovakia, review of legislation by an independent judiciary was squelched in Central Europe.

Thus, at the outset of World War II, the institution of judicial review existed mainly in the Western Hemisphere and functioned vibrantly only in the United States. Since 1945, however, constitutional practice has changed, and judicial review has spread worldwide. This chapter will examine the adoption of this most distinctive of American constitutional practices and also will strive to explain its global acceptance.

Part of the explanation lies in the power and prestige of the United States. Throughout the nineteenth century, Europeans understandably regarded the United States as a cultural and intellectual backwater, and few European legal thinkers paid significant attention to America's legal and constitutional routines. But World War II transformed the position of the United States in the world. Its economic and military prowess commanded respect. Scholars from around the world began to study the legal, political, and constitutional practices of the United States, often at first hand and with financial support from American institutions. And Americans began to advise foreigners who were drafting constitutions or otherwise to participate in the drafting process.

The former Axis powers were among the first to adopt judicial review. The Japanese Constitution of 1946, initially drafted by a committee of Americans in the office of General Douglas MacArthur, the commander of the American occupation army in Japan, explicitly gave the Supreme Court "power to determine the constitutionality of any law, order, regulation or official act," and the court has exercised the power with the observation that it grew out of "interpretation of the American Constitution." Thus, there is little doubt that Japan copied the institution of judicial review from the United States, under the guidance of American thinkers and in the shadow of American military power.

Although Germans drafted the 1949 Constitution of the Federal Republic of Germany—the constitution that remains in force today—American pressure and influence were not absent. As the dominant victor in World War II and the emerging leader of the NATO coalition against the pretensions of the Soviet Union, the United States prodded the drafters of the 1949 constitution to commit Germany to the rule of law under the protection of an independent judiciary. The result was the creation of the Federal Constitutional Tribunal, which during the past half century has become, along with the Supreme Court of the United States, the most activist constitutional court in the world and has rendered some of the most important and interesting decisions of any such court.

Italy had been the third member of the Axis coalition. Although American military power had been highly instrumental in its defeat, Italy, unlike Germany and Japan, was not under military occupation in 1948 when it decided to abolish its monarchy and draft a constitution for a republic. Thus, it is more difficult to pinpoint American influence in the drafting of the 1948 constitution, although the influence was not entirely absent. The Constitution of 1948 explicitly recognized the doctrine of judicial review of the acts of the national legislature, and the establishment of a constitutional court in 1956 brought the practice of judicial review to fruition.

Meanwhile, halfway around the world, the practice of judicial review was also expanding. When India achieved independence from Great Britain in 1947, the framers of its constitution provided for judicial review of acts of the national legislature that violated fundamental individual rights or infringed upon state powers. Neither American prestige nor American military power can explain this development, however. India's elite had been thoroughly indoctrinated with British legal, constitutional, and political ideals, often through attendance at leading English universities, and had little experience with the United States. The American military, which had liberated Italy and conquered Germany and Japan, had no presence whatever in India. Thus, it does not seem that India was adopting judicial review for the purpose of copying the American model.

A better hypothesis is that India embraced judicial review because it served an important need. The subcontinent contains numerous ethnic and religious minorities, which subsequent history has shown had every reason to fear repression at the hands of a national majority dominating the national legislature. Thus, India presented a classic case—a case that would become increasingly frequent as the twentieth century progressed—in which judicial review was needed to protect the integrity and civil liberties of minority races, religions, and other groups.

Canada is another nation with deep ethnic and religious divisions in which judicial review has become vibrant. Canada owes its existence to the British North America Act of 1867, through which the Parliament at Westminster created a federation between the Roman Catholic, French-speaking colony of Quebec and the Protestant, English-speaking colony of Ontario and several smaller provinces. The 1867 act did not, however, give Canada full independence from Great Britain; in particular, the Privy Council in London continued until 1949 to possess jurisdiction to hear appeals from the highest court in Canada.

During the eighty-two years of Privy Council jurisdiction, Canada gained increasing de facto independence, and the Privy Council's role changed imperceptably from one of enforcing Westminster's imperial policies to one of interpreting the North America Act, which had become Canada's constitution. Thus, the Privy Council almost became a court reviewing the constitutionality of the acts of a coordinate legislative branch of government, but since it was a foreign court, sitting in the capital of the former imperial master, it never quite took on that role.

With the end of Privy Council appeals, the Supreme Court of Canada became the ultimate interpreter of the meaning of the North America Act and thus, in effect, the holder of a power of judicial review. It kept a low profile, however, until the Canadian government decided in 1980 to pursue a "patriation" policy of removing all vestiges of British imperial authority from Canadian life, including the vestige that only Parliament in Westminster could amend the Canadian constitution. The Canadian Supreme Court then issued an important ruling on the procedures that the government had to follow in pursuing its policy—a policy that eventuated in the 1982 adoption of a Canadian Charter of Rights and Freedoms.

The Supreme Court of Canada has made the charter a frequent basis for declaring both national and provincial legislation unconstitutional. But the charter gives the Court only a limited power of judicial review, since section 33 of the charter gives both the national and provincial legislatures power to override any court decision. This override has been used only once outside Quebec since 1982 and is, politically speaking, virtually unusable outside that province. But the Quebec assembly has used it with some frequency. Most importantly, when the court struck down a Quebec law requiring French-only advertising signs as a violation of the charter's guarantee of freedom of expression, the Quebec assembly overrode the court's decision.

In cases protecting the rights of women, aborigines, and homosexuals, in contrast, the Canadian Supreme Court has pursued judicial activism with greater success. Together with the actions of the Quebec assembly, these decisions illustrate the essential nature of late-twentieth-century constitutionalism and judicial review. Unlike the constitutionalism proclaimed in *Marbury v. Madison*, that of the late twentieth century concerns the empowerment of discrete and insular ethnic, religious, and cultural minorities. When those minorities possess voting power in legislatures, like the Quebec assembly, contemporary constitutions encourage them to use it to protect their interests. But, when groups lack legislative power, bills of rights and the practice of judicial review of the constitutionality of legislation give them another institution, the judiciary, to provide them with protection.

Another use of a judicial body to deal with ethnic and cultural conflict has occurred in Belgium, which is divided roughly evenly between Flemish-speaking people in the North and French-speaking people in the South. As a result of reforms occurring in 1970 and 1980, Belgium created a Court of Arbitration, consisting of six Flemish-speaking and six French-speaking members, representing the two groups in the nation. In essence, the court has jurisdiction to declare unconstitutional legislation infringing on the reserved rights of either of the groups.

The most recent constitution created for the purpose of protecting a minority is that of South Africa. When the apartheid regime agreed to yield power to a government elected by South Africa's black majority, it did so only on condition that the rights of the white minority be solidly entrenched in the new constitutional order. Many devices in South Africa's constitution entrench white rights and ensure that whites will continue to possess substantial power in the new regime. Here we need to be concerned only with the explicit conferral of power on South Africa's highest court to invalidate legislation that conflicts with rights, especially property rights, protected by the constitution. Through judicial maintenance of their property under the doctrine of judicial review, white South Africans have been made to feel assured that they will not become a powerless minority in their country, even if they are a discrete and insular one.

Thus, the doctrine of judicial review as proclaimed in *Marbury v. Madison* and altered by the United States Supreme Court during the next century and a half began in the aftermath of World War II to spread around the globe. In part, especially in Germany and Japan, American military power and the prestige of the United States as a functioning democratic polity furthered the spread. But it also spread because the Supreme Court's transformation of the doctrine into a device for the protection of ethnic, religious, and cultural minorities gave it a purpose in the late-twentieth-century world order that the original doctrine promulgated in *Marbury* had never enjoyed.

On other occasions during the second half of the twentieth century, judicial review spread for a variety of reasons connected to the specific political needs of the entities adopting it and to a general sense that the experience of the United States demonstrated the doctrine's utility in preserving democratic stability. But explicit pressure from the United States was absent. This was the case in 1950, when the Council of Europe adopted the European Convention for the Protection of Human Rights and Fundamental Freedoms, pursuant to which the European Court of Human Rights was established. It also was true seven years later when the Treaty of Rome created the European Economic Community and endowed it with a supreme judicial body, the European Court of Justice, with jurisdiction to determine whether acts of the EEC's political bodies and acts of member states are consistent with the Community's fundamental charter.

Since the 1950s, many individual nations also have adopted judicial review for reasons connected to their own specific political needs, other than the protection of discrete and insular minorities. France is one of these nations. With the establishment of the Fifth Republic in 1958, France created a Constitutional Council, consisting of nine specially chosen judges plus any living former presidents of the republic. The council is charged with a number of tasks, including the determination of whether legislation is in "conformity with the Constitution . . . before its promulgation."

Other Western European states also have adopted judicial review in one form or another during the past half century. Thus, the Spanish constitution of 1978 reestablished the system of judicial review that had been briefly introduced in the short-lived republican constitution of 1931. The Portuguese constitution of 1976 also adopted judicial review, while Sweden adhered to the practice during the course of the 1970s.

Judicial review finally has penetrated even into the former Communist states of eastern Europe. Yugoslavia created a Constitutional Court, which is now defunct, in 1962. Czechoslovakia established such a court in 1968, and both the Czech Republic and Slovakia continue to maintain constitutional courts today. But the main developments occurred as Communist power collapsed in the late 1980s and early 1990s, and constitutional courts were established in Hungary in 1990, Romania in 1991, Lithuania in 1992, Belarus in 1994, and Latvia and the Ukraine in 1996.

Most important of all was the Constitutional Court created in

Russia in 1991. It has assumed a strongly activist stance, passing on the constitutionality, among other matters, of President Boris Yeltsin's effort to suppress the Chechen rebellion of the mid-1990s and invalidating the legislation requiring Russia's citizens to carry passes while engaged in internal travel. It also appears to have survived Yeltsin's apparent attempt in 1993 to destroy it by forcing the resignation of its presiding judge and packing it with several new judges.

Perhaps the ultimate evidence of the global expansion of judicial review lies in the adoption of bills of rights even by nations that have remained committed to the doctrine of legislative supremacy. New Zealand offers an illustration. In 1985, New Zealand's deputy prime minister proposed adoption of a bill of rights, modeled on the Canadian Charter of Rights and Freedoms, with full-scale, *Marbury*-style judicial review. Opposition to judicial review, however, was strong, and New Zealand finally enacted its new Bill of Rights in 1990 as an ordinary statute, with an explicit provision that it did not render any other legislative enactment void or ineffective. The New Zealand Court of Appeal has obeyed this restriction, but some of its judges nonetheless have found it appropriate to declare some legislation incompatible with the Bill of Rights, even while leaving the legislation in force.

The effect of such declarations of incompatibility is remarkably close to the effect of Canadian declarations of unconstitutionality, which, it will be recalled, are subject to legislative override. In both instances, legislators come under intense political pressure to conform their statute to the requirements of justice—in Canada, by not overriding the judiciary's decision, and in New Zealand, by repealing offending legislation. The difference, of course, is that in Canada the legislature must take action to override, while in New Zealand the legislature must take steps to repeal. Procedurally, this difference sometimes can affect results, but in the end the difference is not fundamental. Both the Canadian and the New Zealand approaches protect ultimate legislative supremacy, while at the same time making it difficult for the legislature to exercise that supremacy.

The ultimate source of the concept of legislative supremacy

is, of course, English constitutional theory. And it is fitting that *Marbury v. Madison* and the doctrine of judicial review may be starting to triumph even in the halls of Westminster, with Parliament's passage of the Human Rights Act of 1998. Like New Zealand's Bill of Rights, Britain's Human Rights Act leaves incompatible legislation in force. But the act, like New Zealand's, does direct judges to strive to interpret other legislation to be consistent with the Human Rights Act, and it also opens the possibility that judges may find it appropriate to declare legislation incompatible, even while leaving it in force. Only time will tell.

CHAPTER 9

The Relevance of *Marbury* to
Judicial Review Today

Should either the doctrine of precedent or fidelity to the intentions of the Founding Fathers compel judges in the twenty-first century to apply *Marbury v. Madison* and the doctrine of judicial review in a narrow, text-bound fashion, which focuses, as nineteenth-century courts did, on the portion of the *Marbury* opinion that invalidated section 13 of the 1789 Judiciary Act on the ground of inconsistency with the text of the Constitution? Or should we understand that judges in constitutional cases have broad power to strike down legislation on the basis of flexible standards of justice protective of discrete and insular minorities and of policies designed to bring those standards of justice to fruition?

Many arguments can be advanced in favor of adhering to precedent and remaining faithful to the original intentions of those who initially created our institutions of government and incorporated their intentions into the written text of the Constitution.

One argument is that Americans who lived in the late eighteenth and early nineteenth centuries possessed proper substantive values and established the Constitution and the federal government on the basis of those values. Americans of that era, it has been said, were Lockean individualists, or alternatively, were Republican communitarians who cared about their fellow citizens' rights and needs. Judges in the twenty-first century, according to this argument, should follow precedent and abide by the intentions of the framing generation because their doing so will ensure our continued governance in accordance with sound substantive values.

A second argument focuses on the personal qualities rather than the substantive values of the framing generation. According to this argument, the men who drafted the Constitution, procured its ratification, and made the early decisions about how to put it into practice were more intelligent and disinterested than the people who ascend to positions of power and authority today. On balance, this greater intelligence and disinterestedness produced better decisions than those that would now be made by judges and political leaders acting on the basis of their own substantive views. It follows that the greater the guidance that today's leaders and judges accept from the past the better their decisions will be.

The third argument—and probably the central one—in favor of adherence to precedent and fidelity to the Founders also provides support for a narrow, text-bound reading of the *Marbury* opinion. This argument does not assume that precedent is good or that the founding generation was somehow superior to the present. Its core instead is that it is illegitimate, in terms of the democratic norms of American political culture, for judges to be making fundamental choices between competing social policies. Two distinct intellectual traditions support this core claim.

The first is legal positivism. Positivists understand law as a set of commands addressed by lawmakers to people, among them judges, who have the capacity to understand and the obligation to obey those commands. Although positivism is under challenge today in many jurisprudential circles, it nonetheless remains difficult to imagine what it would be like to live in a world in which the precepts of positivism—that duly constituted representative bodies of the people have power to issue commands that the people as a whole are bound to obey—did not hold some sway. The precepts underlying positivism still retain great power over our lives and our legal imaginations.

The second tradition is the classical legal convention of judicial neutrality. Judges, it is said, must not favor one party appearing before them over another but rather must treat all litigants in the same way. Indeed, federal judges take an oath to "administer justice without respect to persons, and do equal right to the poor and to the rich." As individual litigants have come to represent the interests of larger groups or classes, it has become equally clear that judges should not show favoritism toward any particular group or class. Above all, it is urged that judges should never derive decisions from their own systems of value or their own preferences for one rather than another social policy.

Judges, the argument continues, are insufficiently attuned to democratic values to make policy choices on behalf of the people. Although politics does play a role in judicial selection processes, federal judges and judges in many states are not elected officials and thus have never had to reveal their policy preferences to the electorate and obtain the electorate's ratification of their policies. Even in states where judges are elected, they almost never reveal how they would decide specific policy questions. Moreover, judges typically hold office for lengthy terms—indeed, in the federal system and in some states, for life or until retirement. By the time judges are nearing the end of their term in office, it is thought, they have grown even more distant from popular, democratic processes of policy choice. The end result, it is feared, is that judges will make social policy choices without regard to the wishes of the electorate, and the democratic norm that the people themselves should determine the laws and policies by which they are governed will be defeated.

Sophisticated theorists who argue in favor of adherence to precedent and fidelity to the framers do not doubt that judges on some occasions must make some policy choices and that the choices they make sometimes will preclude the democratic political process from making other choices. Sophisticated theorists understand that, in creating precedent, judges inevitably make choices—that when judges engage in common-law decision making in contract and tort cases, for example, they engage in interstitial policy making. But, the theorists add, the legislature has the capacity by a simple majority vote to overturn the judiciary's policy choice in such cases, and its failure to vote to overturn can be understood as a sort of tacit, democratic acceptance of the choice the judges had made.

Similarly, theorists who argue in favor of fidelity to the framers understand that judicial obedience to the past may preclude present, democratic majorities from making the policy choices they now desire. Since the Constitution, for instance, outlaws slavery, the people could not vote to reestablish the practice of slavery or direct Congress or the state legislatures to do so, no matter how much a majority of them may want the practice reinstated. Such theorists emphasize, however, that it is not the policy choice of judges that is preventing a present democratic majority from enacting the policies it desires; it is a past, democratic, supermajority that is preventing the current democratic majority from enacting certain laws. And it is noted that if a present, democratic, supermajority wanted to do so, it could change the Constitution, overturn what the past supermajority had decided, and abolish the limits it had imposed.

John Marshall, as we have seen, incorporated many of these values into his *Marbury v. Madison* opinion. In light of his training in eighteenth-century legal and political theory, he fully appreciated the view of nearly all Americans that judges should not decide contested issues of social policy. The only proper role for judges, according to the logic of the *Marbury* opinion, is to follow established common law rules, to follow legislation when it alters the common law, and to follow the Constitution if it conflicts with legislation. If they adhere to such a role, judges will never decide policy issues but will only give effect to past decisions in which the people have acquiesced either through the legislative process or through their sovereign role as constitution makers.

Such an interpretation of *Marbury v. Madison* thus incorporates some very basic assumptions about American law and politics. On this interpretation of *Marbury*, it is impossible to make any sense of John Marshall's opinion or of judicial review except against a background assumption that the duty of judges, especially in constitutional cases, is to decide questions of law and abstain from politics. On this reading, judges are obliged to avoid policy issues, to defer to the legislature when they arise, and to invalidate legislation as unconstitutional only if they can ground their judgment in the text of the Constitution or in the clear intentions of its framers.

Marbury itself, as we have seen, arguably can be defended as a case in which the Supreme Court avoided policy issues, focused on the text of the Constitution, and thus rendered a legal, as distinguished from a political, decision. It is also possible to defend property rights cases as late as the end of the nineteenth century as involving mere protection of established legal rights codified by the Constitution's text in the Fifth and Fourteenth Amendments. Although the property rights cases, from the perspective of progressive reformers, involved policy choice, the justices who decided them could have viewed them as applying nothing more than established law.

Problems exist, however, with this narrow form of judicial review emphasizing only adherence to precedent and fidelity to the text of the Constitution and the intentions of its framers. One problem is that judicial review, in this narrow form, possesses little of the political and social signficance that we have come to attribute to it. For instance, the section of 1789 Judiciary Act invalidated in *Marbury*, which had granted the Supreme Court the power to issue writs of mandamus as a matter of original jurisdiction, simply is unimportant; both litigants and the Court are equally well served by a practice that permits lower courts to grant writs, subject to the possibility of an appeal to the Supreme Court. Many early-nineteenth-century judicial review cases in state courts involved equally insignificant housekeeping legislation.

A second problem is that the narrow form of judicial review practiced in early-nineteenth-century America was irrelevant to the rest of the world. Other nations did not need a judiciary to serve as a bulwark of property rights against redistributive onslaughts from the political left—the most significant function that the doctrine performed in the United States. In most of nineteenth-century Europe, in contrast, a monarch, a hereditary nobility, and an established church, all with extensive landholdings, were able to protect their own property rights as well as the entrepreneurial rights of the growing bourgeoisie. Europeans in the nineteenth century did not need *Marbury* and hence did not adopt judicial review, nor can we understand that they and other nations in the world need judicial review today in order to protect property. The global expansion of judicial review can be explained only if we understand that the doctrine serves broader social purposes than it did in nineteenth-century America.

Thus there is a need for a broader reading of *Marbury*, and it is fortunate that the narrow reading is not the only possible one. The case need not be read to define constitutional law only as a body of positivist commands by the sovereign people—commands that have been incorporated into the text of the Constitution. While it might sometimes be useful so to define constitutional law, especially in nations with recently adopted constitutions that, like the new constitution of South Africa, codify certain specific rights, the definition is not the only one that is available. Chief Justice Marshall also can be understood in *Marbury* to have defined constitutional law as giving authority to the Supreme Court of the United States and to other constitutional courts throughout the world to identify and enforce, even against majoritarian legislation, values widely shared by the people as a whole.

Marbury's ambiguity lies in the fact that one part of the opinion finds law in the text of the Constitution, while another part finds it in the consensus of the people. Of course, the Supreme Court found that it could not grant William Marbury the remedy he sought because a close reading of the Constitution's text denied it jurisdiction and trumped a contrary act of Congress. But earlier it had found that Marbury had a right to his commission because, by the consensus of American lawyers, a commission for office was a property right and because, by the consensus of the American people, property was a fundamental, legal right that trumped the political will of the popular majority that had just placed a new presidential administration in power.

Judicial review is important today because it gives effect to a consensus that began to emerge in the late 1930s and that since then has become widely shared by Americans and most other people in the world: a consensus that racial, religious, and comparable forms of discrimination are profoundly evil and unjust. Hitler, the Holocaust, and genocide have become humanity's paradigms of iniquity. And judicial review has become the institutional mechanism through which people can advance policies that promote justice and equality and prevent injustice and discrimination.

Brown v. Board of Education, which declared invalid statutes enacted by Southern state legislatures that mandated segregation in public schools, is the twentieth-century case that illustrates the new form of judicial review at its best. In *Brown,* the Supreme Court rejected the narrow version of judicial review focusing on adherence to precedent, framers' intentions, and the Constitution's text. Adherence to precedent probably would have required the Court to affirm the 1896 case of *Plessy v. Ferguson,* which had upheld the constitutionality of segregated facilities as long as they were equal. *Plessy,* in turn, had been decided as it was because the relevant constitutional text—namely, the Fourteenth Amendment—requires equal protection but does not address the question whether equal, segregated facilities satisfy its requirement.

In light of the ambiguity of the constitutional text, the Court in *Brown* appears to have hoped that analysis of the intentions of the framers of the Fourteenth Amendment would help it to decide the segregation issue. Accordingly, it requested the litigants to brief the question whether the framers intended the amendment to prohibit segregation in public schools. But in the end, the Court concluded that these intentions were too indefinite to answer the constitutional question before it.

Adherence to precedent and fidelity to the framers was simply trumped in *Brown* by a variety of intelletual and societal developments in the middle of the twentieth century that compelled the Court to take a new approach and overrule *Plessy.* The development of an increasingly powerful African-American middle class, the attainment of social and economic equality by Catholic and Jewish immigrant groups, American revulsion at Nazi racism, and the emergence of the Third World all contributed to the collapse of the late nineteenth century's neo-Darwinian hierarchical conception of the relationship between the world's ethnic groups and to a growing consensus in favor of an end to racial discrimination.

There can be little doubt, for example, that African Americans at the middle of the twentieth century saw their treatment in

America as different only in degree from the treatment accorded Jews in Nazi Germany. It also seems clear that they saw their drive for equality as analogous to similar efforts by Catholic and Jewish minorities. It is difficult to question the soundness of this black perspective. While white Americans were able to ignore the black perspective before it was brought to their attention, they were unable, once made aware of it, to advance coherent counterarguments, because nearly all Americans in 1954 viewed the fall of fascism, the end of colonialism, and the entrance of Catholics and Jews into the social mainstream as inevitable, if not positively beneficial, developments.

The emerging consensus against various forms of discrimination thus gave rise to a persuasive argument in support of *Brown*'s outlawing of racial discrimination. The argument was that because the nation had embraced the principle of racial and religious equality—by fighting a global war against fascism and admitting Catholics and Jews into the mainstream of society—it could not in all fairness object to the application of that same principle to African-American schoolchildren. Given the premise that legal principles are to be applied evenhandedly to all who are similarly situated, it seemed impossible to justify the segregation of African Americans without also authorizing the segregation of other racial and ethnic groups—like the Jews in Nazi Germany—that lack the power to protect themselves in the political process.

Of course, the white South opposed the result reached by the Warren Court in *Brown*. Most white Southerners in 1954 wanted to continue the practice of racial segregation. But they were not prepared to translate their emotional self-interest into a principled argument in support of the practice. The coherent argument in opposition to *Brown* was that of Aryan supremacy, but to make that argument, one would have had to insult the emerging Third World, deny the right of American Catholics and Jews to equality, and ultimately embrace fascism. Because the white Southerners who opposed desegregation were not fascists, they never offered this argument in *Brown*. As a result, they were unable to explain why the nation's policies toward African Americans should be different from its policies toward other non-Aryan groups, but were forced instead to ask that racial segregation be continued simply because it suited their own interests.

It is important to emphasize what has just been said for what it reveals about the nature of principled, consensus-based judicial decision making, whether in the eighteenth century or today. There will always be individuals and groups whose interests do not coincide with the interests of the majority. It remained in the interests of many whites, for example, to continue exploiting African Americans in the mid-twentieth-century South. But litigants cannot appear before judges and simply announce that their interests demand a particular decision; the litigants also must make principled arguments.

One possible argument is that the law—the body of doctrine derived from precedent or enacted by the sovereign—justifies the desired decision. Chief Justice John Marshall recognized and legitimated such arguments in *Marbury v. Madison.* A second possible argument is that the publicly proclaimed values on which the community agrees, as articulated by juries in the eighteenth century or by societal leaders and the media today, constitute a second form of law on which it is equally appropriate for a court to rely in reaching decisions. Marshall also recognized and legitimated arguments of this sort in *Marbury.*

An intellectual movement within the legal academy, which its proponents labeled critical legal studies, has maintained that consensus of the sort on which, I argue, Marshall relied is impossible, because smart lawyers can always advance arguments outside its bounds that will cause it to collapse. Of course, it is true that no shared premises can exist outside some context capable of conferring meaning. No case can be resolved on the basis of a consensus about premises if all possible arguments in support of all possible outcomes are presented to judges. The contexts in which cases arise, however, limit the arguments to which the judges will give serious consideration and which the litigants therefore can plausibly present.

The point about *Brown,* for instance, is that its context—the fact that it came before the Supreme Court less than a decade after World War II had obliterated three fascist dictatorships—

rendered implausible the strongest arguments in favor of continuing racial segregation. Virtually all Americans accepted the set of liberal, egalitarian premises for which the war had been fought, and the legal arguments derived from those neutral premises cut decisively in favor of the result in *Brown*.

Consensus, then, does not require a set of values that advances everyone's interest or that everyone accepts. There will be extremists, who lie outside the mainstream or center of society, who proclaim contrary values, and everyone at some point in time will probably feel that existing values conflict with their interests. There were Tories in 1776 and white supremacists in 1954, but we nevertheless feel comfortable proclaiming that the American people demanded independence in 1776 and racial equality in 1954. At least in historical retrospect, we can see that the mainstream of society had coalesced around particular values in the contexts of 1776 and 1954 and that those individuals who did not agree had been pushed outside the mainstream and into the extreme.

Noncoercive democratic societies cannot exist without at least some agreement on values—without at least some consensus. That consensus may be either broad or narrow, depending on the particular historical context. People will disagree about what the consensus is, and it will sometimes be possible, at least in the hindsight of history, to report that particular efforts to explicate a consensus were right or wrong.

Thus, when judges try to identify a consensus on which to base a decision, they will, of course, sometimes be mistaken. They should be criticized for their mistakes, just as they are criticized when they misapprehend the law. But they should not be criticized for striving to find a consensus and for basing their decision on it. Criticism from the political left, which says that no consensus exists, should be understood for what it is—a claim that noncoercive democracy no longer exists. And criticism from the political right, which says that adherence to precedent and fidelity to the Founding Fathers permits only a narrow, text-bound version of constitutional adjudication, should be understood as a careless, myopic reading of *Marbury v. Madison*, which fails to recognize that the opinion addresses many issues and resolves them on many grounds.

There remains one difficulty. To the extent that a consensus is hazy or ambiguous, people will have competing policy visions about how it should be applied, and judges who rely on the consensus as the foundation for their decisions may be forced to choose among the competing visions. In the view of eighteenth-century thinkers, judges had no jurisdiction to make policy choices, and those who believe that this eighteenth-century vision was codified in *Marbury* or the Constitution will find judicial policy making troublesome.

It is not clear, however, that either John Marshall or eighteenth-century judges were deterred from consensus decision making by a concern that policy choice would be required at the margins. The opinions of the Marshall Court and those of earlier eighteenth-century courts were not always unanimous. Moreover, Marshall and earlier judges understood that the social center of gravity could change, and they participated in the process of change. For example, nearly all colonials who later became Tories shared a consensus with other Americans in 1765 about the unconstitutionality of the Stamp Act, but as the marginal issue of how to protect American constitutional rights became increasingly central during the course of the next decade and a new consensus around independence emerged, the Tories found themselves left at the extreme.

Policy choice, moreover, simply may be inevitable. A conclusion of this book is that Americans and most other people of the world agree that racial, religious, and comparable forms of discrimination are profoundly evil and unjust. They also seem to understand that legislatures chosen through majoritarian, democratic processes sometimes lack the impartiality to provide the necessary protection that victims of discrimination deserve. Only judges are sufficiently insulated from majority prejudices to be trusted.

But there are two subsidiary matters about which Americans and the people of the world do not agree. They do not agree about how to achieve racial, religious, or any other form of equality. Nor do they agree about whether other forms of discrimination, such as discrimination on the basis of sexual orientation, are comparable to racial and religious discrimination.

Judges inevitably must make policy judgments about these and other subsidiary issues as they provide discrete and insular minorities with the protection against discrimination that justice demands. The effect of arguments against judicial policy making, if those arguments are heeded, will be to free judges from any constitutional duty to provide such protection. Arguments against judicial policy making, if heeded, will leave minorities subject to the whims and prejudices of democratic majorities. As we listen to and evaluate the arguments, we thus need to weigh which of two competing values—fidelity to a particular one of several possible readings of *Marbury v. Madison* or allegiance to the principle of human equality and nondiscrimination—is more important. At least this much policy choice is inevitable.

BIBLIOGRAPHICAL ESSAY

Note from the Series Editors: The following bibliographical essay contains the major primary and secondary sources the author consulted for this volume. We have asked all authors in the series to omit formal citations in order to make our volumes more readable, inexpensive, and appealing for students and general readers. In adopting this format, Landmark Law Cases and American Society follows the precedent of a number of highly regarded and widely consulted series.

Marbury v. Madison is reported at 1 Cranch (5 U.S.) 137 (1803). For classic interpretations of the case by progressive historians, *see* Albert J. Beveridge, *The Life of John Marshall*, 4 vols. (Boston: Houghton Mifflin, 1916–1919); Felix Frankfurter, *The Commerce Clause under Marshall, Taney and Waite* (Chapel Hill: University of North Carolina Press, 1937); and Charles Warren, *The Supreme Court in United States History*, 2 vols. (Boston: Little Brown, 1922). For more recent interpretations in the same mold, *see* Robert G. McCloskey, *The American Supreme Court* (Chicago: University of Chicago Press, 1960); J. M. Sosin, *The Aristocracy of the Long Robe: The Origins of Judicial Review in America* (Westport, Conn.: Greenwood Press, 1989); and Christopher L. Eisgruber, "John Marshall's Judicial Rhetoric," *1996 Supreme Court Review* (Chicago: University of Chicago Press, 1997), 439.

Most recent scholarship, however, tends to place the *Marbury* decision in the context of late-eighteenth- and early-nineteenth-century politics and ideas. Three classic works on mid- to late-eighteenth-century political theory are Bernard Bailyn, *The Ideological Origins of the American Revolution* (Cambridge, Mass.: Harvard University Press, 1967); John Phillip Reid, *Constitutional History of the American Revolution* (Madison: University of Wisconsin Press, 1995); and Gordon S. Wood, *The Creation of the American Republic, 1776–1787* (Chapel Hill: University of North Carolina Press, 1969). The scholarship during the past two decades that places *Marbury* in the theoretical context elucidated by these books includes Robert Lowry Clinton, Marbury v. Madison *and Judicial Review* (Lawrence: University Press of Kansas, 1989); Charles F. Hobson, *The Great Chief Justice:*

John Marshall and the Rule of Law (Lawrence: University Press of Kansas, 1996); Sylvia Snowiss, *Judicial Review and the Law of the Constitution* (New Haven: Yale University Press, 1990); James M. O'Fallon, "Marbury," *Stanford Law Review* 44 (1992): 219; and William E. Nelson, "The Eighteenth-Century Background of John Marshall's Constitutional Jurisprudence," *Michigan Law Review* 76 (1978): 893.

A vast literature exists in regard to the social structure of the localities of eighteenth-century British North America. The best work includes T. H. Breen, *Tobacco Culture: The Mentality of the Great Planters on the Eve of Revolution* (Princeton: Princeton University Press, 1985); Edward M. Cook Jr., *The Fathers of the Towns: Leadership and Community Structure in Eighteenth-Century New England* (Baltimore: Johns Hopkins University Press, 1976); Edward Countryman, *A People in Revolution: The American Revolution and Political Society in New York, 1760–1790* (Baltimore: Johns Hopkins University Press, 1981); Rhys Isaac, *The Transformation of Virginia, 1740–1790* (Chapel Hill: University of North Carolina Press, 1982); Rachel N. Klein, *Unification of a Slave State: The Rise of the Planter Class in the South Carolina Backcountry, 1760–1808* (Chapel Hill: University of North Carolina Press, 1990); Gary B. Nash, *The Urban Crucible: Social Change, Political Consciousness, and the Origins of the American Revolution* (Cambridge, Mass.: Harvard University Press, 1979); William M. Offutt, *Law and Society in the Delaware Valley, 1680–1710* (Champaign: University of Illinois Press, 1995); Darrett B. Rutman and Anita H. Rutman, *A Place in Time: Middlesex County, Virginia, 1650–1750* (New York: W. W. Norton, 1984); and Michael Zuckerman, *Peaceable Kingdoms: New England Towns in the Eighteenth Century* (New York: Alfred A. Knopf, 1970).

On the role of eighteenth-century courts and juries in the context of this social structure, I have relied mainly on my own earlier work, William E. Nelson, "The Eighteenth-Century Background of John Marshall's Constitutional Jurisprudence," *Michigan Law Review* 76 (1978): 893, and William E. Nelson, *Americanization of the Common Law: The Impact of Legal Change on Massachusetts Society, 1760–1830* (Cambridge, Mass.: Harvard University Press, 1975), but also on F. Thornton Miller, *Juries and Judges versus the Law: Virginia's Provincial Legal Perspective, 1783–1828* (Charlottesville: University Press of Virginia, 1994); Gwenda Morgan, *The Hegemony of the Law: Rich-*

mond County, Virginia, 1692–1776 (New York: Garland Publishing, 1989); and Deborah A. Rosen, *Courts and Commerce: Gender, Law and the Market Economy in Colonial New York* (Columbus: Ohio State University Press, 1997). For reasons stated in the Preface to the 1994 edition of William E. Nelson, *Americanization of the Common Law: The Impact of Legal Change on Massachusetts Society, 1760–1830* (Athens: University of Georgia Press, 1994), at xii–xiii, I continue to reject the position of Bruce H. Mann, *Neighbors and Strangers: Law and Community in Early Connecticut* (Chapel Hill: University of North Carolina Press, 1987), that the power of juries to find law as well as fact declined in the early and mid-eighteenth century.

Two recent books that together provide the best overview of government and politics for the entire 1760–1800 period are Robert Middlekauff, *The Glorious Cause: The American Revolution, 1763–1789* (New York: Oxford University Press, 1982), and Stanley Elkins and Eric McKitrick, *The Age of Federalism: The Early American Republic, 1788–1800* (New York: Oxford University Press, 1993). For the period leading up to the War for Independence, Bernard Bailyn, *The Ideological Origins of the American Revolution* (Cambridge, Mass.: Harvard University Press, 1967), and Merrill Jensen, *The Founding of a Nation: A History of the American Revolution* (New York: Oxford University Press, 1968), remain vital and offer competing interpretations. On the war years themselves, Piers Mackesy, *The War for America, 1775–1783* (Cambridge, Mass.: Harvard University Press, 1964), and Charles Royster, *A Revolutionary People at War: The Continental Army and American Character, 1775–1783* (Chapel Hill: University of North Carolina Press, 1979), are recommended. For the Confederation period, *see* Merrill Jensen, *The Articles of Confederation* (Madison: University of Wisconsin Press, 1940), and Jack N. Rakove, *The Beginnings of National Politics: An Interpretive History of the Continental Congress* (New York: Alfred A. Knopf, 1979), again for differing interpretations. On the process leading up to the adoption of the federal Constitution, three classics are Max Farrand, *The Framing of the Constitution of the United States* (New Haven: Yale University Press, 1913); Forrest McDonald, *We the People: The Economic Origins of the Constitution* (Chicago: University of Chicago Press, 1958), and Gordon Wood, *The Creation of the American Republic, 1776–1787* (Chapel Hill: University of North Carolina Press, 1969). On early judicial review in the states, *see* William E. Nelson, "Changing Conceptions of Judicial Review: The Evolution of Constitutional Theory in the States," *University of Pennsylvania Law Review* 120 (1972): 1166.

For some of the vast literature on government and politics in the 1790s, *see* Jerald A. Combs, *The Jay Treaty: Political Battleground of the Founding Fathers* (Berkeley: University of California Press, 1970); Noble E. Cunningham, *The Jeffersonian Republicans: The Formation of Party Organization, 1789–1801* (Chapel Hill: University of North Carolina Press, 1957); Manning J. Dauer, *The Adams Federalists* (Baltimore: Johns Hopkins University Press, 1953); E. James Ferguson, *The Power of the Purse: A History of American Public Finance, 1776–1790* (Chapel Hill: University of North Carolina Press, 1961); David C. Hendrickson, *Empire of Liberty: The Statecraft of Thomas Jefferson* (New York: Oxford University Press, 1990); Richard Hofstadter, *The Idea of a Party System: The Rise of Legitimate Opposition in the United States, 1780–1840* (Berkeley: University of California Press, 1969); Stephen G. Kurtz, *The Presidency of John Adams: The Collapse of Federalism, 1795–1800* (Philadelphia: University of Pennsylvania Press, 1957); Forrest McDonald, *Alexander Hamilton: A Biography* (New York: W. W. Norton, 1979); Clinton Rossiter, *Alexander Hamilton and the Constitution* (New York: Harcourt, Brace and World, 1964); and Leonard D. White, *The Federalists: A Study in Administrative History* (New York: Macmillan, 1948).

A different body of scholarship addresses the life of John Marshall, the author of *Marbury v. Madison*. The classic biography of Marshall is Albert J. Beveridge, *The Life of John Marshall*, 4 vols. (Boston: Houghton Mifflin, 1916–1919). The three most recent biographical treatments are Charles F. Hobson, *The Great Chief Justice: John Marshall and the Rule of Law* (Lawrence: University Press of Kansas, 1996); Herbert A. Johnson, *The Chief Justiceship of John Marshall* (Columbia: University of South Carolina Press, 1997); and Jean Edward Smith, *John Marshall: Definer of a Nation* (New York: Henry Holt, 1996). Hobson's treatment is especially valuable, since Hobson is the editor of the John Marshall papers and he has included and discussed in his biography references to sources unused by previous biographers and historians. Two other useful biographies are Leonard Baker, *John Marshall: A Life in Law* (New York: Macmillan, 1974), and Francis N.

Stites, *John Marshall: Defender of the Constitution* (Boston: Little, Brown and Co., 1981).

The companion case to *Marbury*, which is *Stuart v. Laird*, is reported at 5 U.S. (1 Cranch) 299 (1803). The *Marbury* case, and to a lesser extent, the *Stuart* case, have been the subjects of an enormous scholarly commentary. I have relied most heavily on my own article, William E. Nelson, "The Eighteenth-Century Background of John Marshall's Constitutional Jurisprudence," *Michigan Law Review* 76 (1978): 893, as well as on Robert Lowry Clinton, Marbury v. Madison *and Judicial Review* (Lawrence: University Press of Kansas, 1989); Donald O. Dewey, *Marshall versus Jefferson: The Political Background of Marbury v. Madison* (New York: Alfred A. Knopf, 1970); George L. Haskins and Herbert A. Johnson, *Foundations of Power: John Marshall, 1801–15* (New York: Macmillan, 1981); Charles F. Hobson, *The Great Chief Justice: John Marshall and the Rule of Law* (Lawrence: University Press of Kansas, 1996); Jean Edward Smith, *John Marshall: Definer of a Nation* (New York: Henry Holt, 1996); Sylvia Snowiss, *Judicial Review and the Law of the Constitution* (New Haven: Yale University Press, 1990); J. M. Sosin, *The Aristocracy of the Long Robe: The Origins of Judicial Review in America* (Westport, Conn.: Greenwood Press, 1989); and William Van Alstyne, "A Critical Guide to *Marbury v. Madison*," *Duke Law Journal* 15 (1969): 1.

On the conflict between Federalists and Antifederalists, and later Federalists and Republicans, over the scope and power of the federal judiciary—the conflict at the root of *Marbury* and *Stuart*—see Saul Cornell, *The Other Founders: Anti-Federalism and the Dissenting Tradition in America, 1788–1828* (Chapel Hill: University of North Carolina Press, 1999); and Richard E. Ellis, *The Jeffersonian Crisis: Courts and Politics in the Young Republic* (New York: Oxford University Press, 1971).

The best discussion of the immediate reception of the *Marbury* case is contained in Jean Edward Smith, *John Marshall: Definer of a Nation* (New York: Henry Holt, 1996). For the impact of *Marbury* during the course of the nineteenth century's first two decades, I have relied most heavily on my own article, William E. Nelson, "The Eighteenth-Century Background of John Marshall's Constitutional Jurisprudence," *Michigan Law Review* 76 (1978): 893, as well as on

Robert Lowry Clinton, *Marbury v. Madison and Judicial Review* (Lawrence: University Press of Kansas, 1989); George L. Haskins and Herbert A. Johnson, *Foundations of Power: John Marshall, 1801–15* (New York: Macmillan, 1981); Charles F. Hobson, *The Great Chief Justice: John Marshall and the Rule of Law* (Lawrence: University Press of Kansas, 1996); and J. M. Sosin, *The Aristocracy of the Long Robe: The Origins of Judicial Review in America* (Westport, Conn.: Greenwood Press, 1989). For analysis of judicial review in state courts in the late eighteenth and early nineteenth centuries, see William E. Nelson, "Changing Conceptions of Judicial Review: The Evolution of Constitutional Theory in the States, 1790–1860," *University of Pennsylvania Law Review* 120 (1972): 1166, and the classic essay of James B. Thayer, "The Origin and Scope of the American Doctrine of Constitutional Law," *Harvard Law Review* 7 (1893): 129.

For analysis of the longer history of judicial review over the course of the nineteenth century, I have relied mainly on my own earlier work: William E. Nelson, *The Roots of American Bureaucracy, 1830–1900* (Cambridge, Mass.: Harvard University Press, 1982); William E. Nelson, "The Eighteenth-Century Background of John Marshall's Constitutional Jurisprudence," *Michigan Law Review* 76 (1978): 893; and William E. Nelson, "Changing Conceptions of Judicial Review: The Evolution of Constitutional Theory in the States, 1790–1860," *University of Pennsylvania Law Review* 120 (1972): 1166. I continue to find Arnold M. Paul, *Conservative Crisis and the Rule of Law: Attitudes of Bench and Bar, 1887–1895* (Ithaca: Cornell University Press, 1960), valuable. Other useful work includes James W. Ely Jr., *The Guardian of Every Other Right: A Constitutional History of Property Rights* (New York: Oxford University Press, 1992); Benjamin F. Wright, *The Growth of American Constitutional Law* (New York: Reynal and Hitchcock, 1942); Edward S. Corwin, "The Doctrine of Due Process before the Civil War," *Harvard Law Review* 24 (1911): 366, 460; Edward S. Corwin, "The Basic Doctrine of American Constitutional Law," *Michigan Law Review* 12 (1914): 247; and Charles G. Haines, "Judicial Review of Legislation in the United States and the Doctrine of Vested Rights and of Implied Limitations on Legislatures," *Texas Law Review* 2 (1924): 257, 387; 3 (1924): 1.

Historians have long debated whether a sudden change occurred in the jurisprudence of the United States Supreme Court in the late

1930s, what the nature of that change was, and why the change occurred. For recent variants of the conventional wisdom, which sees a conservative Supreme Court buckling under pressure from a liberal president and suddenly transforming its jurisprudence in the spring of 1937, *see* William E. Leuchtenburg, *The Supreme Court Reborn* (New York: Oxford University Press, 1995); Michael Ariens, "A Thrice-Told Tale, or Felix the Cat," *Harvard Law Review* 107 (1994): 620; Richard D. Friedman, "A Reaffirmation: The Authenticity of the Roberts Memorandum, or Felix the Non-Forger," *University of Pennsylvania Law Review* 142 (1994): 1985; and Richard D. Friedman, "Switching Time and Other Thought Experiments: The Hughes Court and Constitutional Transformation," *University of Pennsylvania Law Review* 142 (1994): 1891. Bruce A. Ackerman, *We the People: Transformations* (Cambridge, Mass.: Harvard University Press, 1998), builds a complex argument that the 1937 change was so momentous that it enjoys the stature of a constitutional amendment. In contrast, Barry Cushman, *Rethinking the New Deal Court: The Structure of a Constitutional Revolution* (New York: Oxford University Press, 1998), argues that the change in the Court's jurisprudence was a gradual one, beginning in the 1920s and ending in the 1940s, that was more in the nature of common law accretion than constitutional transformation. Only two articles situate the jurisprudential changes of 1937–1938 in the context of Nazism in Europe and American reactions to Nazism, as I do here. *See* Robert M. Cover, "The Origins of Judicial Activism in the Protection of Minorities," *Yale Law Journal* 91 (1982): 1287; William E. Nelson, "The Changing Meaning of Equality in Twentieth-Century Constitutional Law," *Washington and Lee Law Review* 52 (1995): 3.

Many books have examined the global spread of judicial review. The old standard is Mauro Cappelletti, *Judicial Review in the Contemporary World* (Indianapolis: Bobbs-Merrill, 1971), but so many developments have occurred since its publication that it is now badly out-of-date. The most thorough recent book, which, however, also is becoming dated, is Allan R. Brewer-Carias, *Judicial Review in Comparative Law* (Cambridge: Cambridge University Press, 1989). More recent books of value include Rob Bakker, Aalt Willem Heringa, and Frits Stroink, eds., *Judicial Control: Comparative Essays on Judicial Review* (Apeldoorn, Netherlands: Maklu, 1995); David M. Beatty, ed.,

Human Rights and Judicial Review: A Comparative Perspective (Dordrecht: Martinus Nijhoff, 1994); Donald W. Jakson and C. Neal Tate, eds., *Comparative Judicial Review and Public Policy* (Westport, Conn.: Greenwood Press, 1992); C. Neal Tate and Torbjorn Vallinder, *The Global Expansion of Judicial Power* (New York: New York University Press, 1995); Edward McWhinney, *Supreme Courts and Judicial Law-Making: Constitutional Tribunals and Constitutional Review* (Dordrecht: Martinus Nijhoff, 1986). For some very recent developments, *see* Matthew Harris, "A Bill of Rights without *Marbury:* The Limits of Judicial Review under the New Zealand Bill of Rights" (unpublished paper in possession of author). Barry Turner, ed., *The Statesman's Year-Book: The Essential Political and Economic Guide to All the Countries of the World, 1998–1999*, 135th ed. (New York: St. Martin's Press, 1998), contains a useful, although occasionally incomplete, nation-by-nation account of the constitutional courts that currently exist throughout the world.

Marbury v. Madison has enormous continuing significance to contemporary American constitutional law and constitutional theory. It is almost impossible to open a volume of a contemporary law review without finding at least one article addressed, at least tangentially, to the issue of how judges should decide constitutional cases. My own thinking on this issue was developed in William E. Nelson, "History and Neutrality in Constitutional Adjudication, *Virginia Law Review* 72 (1986): 1237, and my views on constitutional adjudication are derived from that article.

Several recent works, which also provide additional bibliographic guidance, are Antonin Scalia, Amy Gutmann, Gordon S. Wood, Laurence H. Tribe, Mary Ann Glendon, and Ronald Dworkin, *A Matter of Interpretation: Federal Courts and the Law* (Princeton: Princeton University Press, 1997); Christopher L. Eisgruber, "Early Interpretations and Original Sins," *Michigan Law Review* 95 (1997): 2005; Barry Friedman and Scott B. Smith, "The Sedimentary Constitution," *University of Pennsylvania Law Review* 147 (1998): 1; Michael W. McConnell, "The Importance of Humility in Judicial Review: A Comment on Ronald Dworkin's 'Moral Reading' of the Constitution," *Fordham Law Review* 65 (1997): 1269. Most noteworthy among the classic works are John Hart Ely, *Democracy and Distrust: A Theory of Judicial Review* (Cambridge, Mass.: Harvard University Press, 1980);

Robert H. Bork, "Neutral Principles and Some First Amendment Problems," *Indiana Law Journal* 47 (1971): 1; Paul Brest, "The Misconceived Quest for the Original Understanding," *Boston University Law Review* 60 (1980): 204; Michael J. Perry, "Interpretivism, Freedom of Expression, and Equal Protection," *Ohio State Law Journal* 42 (1981): 261; H. Jefferson Powell, "The Original Understanding of Original Intent," *Harvard Law Review* 98 (1985): 885; Mark V. Tushnet, "Following the Rules Laid Down: A Critique of Interpretivism and Neutral Principles," *Harvard Law Review* 96 (1983): 781; Herbert Wechsler, "Toward Neutral Principles of Constitutional Law," *Harvard Law Review* 73 (1959): 1.

INDEX